DIVIDEND INVESTING

*A Beginner's Guide for Income Growth
Finding Your Way to Financial Freedom.
Stock Dividends Made Easy*

Patrick Neilson

Table of Contents

Introduction

Thank you for taking the time to read this book and congratulations on becoming a leader with your finances!

In this book, we are going to teach you about one of the oldest and surest ways to grow your wealth and income over the years, Dividend Investing. While it takes time and discipline, building a portfolio of stocks that pay dividends is one of the best ways to guarantee an income in retirement, or before retirement. When you develop a program of dividend investing, you will use the power of compound interest in order to grow an income-generating portfolio that can help you to live in comfort and security for many decades. Depending on how much you invest over the years, you can even build substantial wealth and generate a high income in the coming decades.

This book is aimed at beginning investors, and so we are assuming that you are brand new to the topic. So we'll begin the book by explaining what dividend stocks are and how they work.

From here, we'll explore the why of dividend investing. You will learn about the power of compound interest, and why it is better to use it with stocks rather than a savings account or other banking instruments. We'll also talk about the tax implications of dividend investing, and if you are new to the concept of individually directed investing, we'll teach you how to choose the best brokerage.

Then we'll teach you about the common strategies the pros like Warren Buffett use to build a winning portfolio. You'll learn how to create a properly diversified stock portfolio, dollar-cost averaging, and other strategies. We will also discuss exchange trade and mutual funds, along with IRA accounts, and how these might fit into a dividend investing plan.

Dividend investing is a powerful way to build wealth, and it has been used by the financially savvy to secure their retirements—literally for centuries. I hope that this book will help you join the ranks of the financially savvy so that you can build your own secure fountain of wealth!

Please keep in mind that this book is for educational purposes only. It is not to be taken as investment advice, and we are not advising you to invest in stocks or any particular stock or fund. Past performance is not a guarantee of future returns, and remember that all investments carry the risk of complete loss of capital.

The Key to Success of the Investor: Mindset

Mindset dictates how we handle situations and is made up of assumptions and judgments. Our mindset is affected by our conscious, subconscious, and unconscious minds.The basic organization of these levels of our psyche fit together in way in which mindset affects each. We make judgments according to our mindset. For example, you may be happy about one thing while the person next to you is sad about the same thing. Our mindset is made up of our brain's communication with the outside world, memories, and experiences. It is the latter two that shape our beliefs and habits, forming our behavior. However, this is not a dissertation on cognitive psychology so will stick to the topic of how mindset can make a positive difference in your approach to investing in the stock market.

Robert Kiyosakisaid, "It's not how much money you make, but how much money you keep, how hard it works for you, and how many generations you keep it for."So the first step is set your intention at the onset of your investing activities and keep a positive mindset. You have to be willing to succeed and take risks. The investors who have a positive mindset are letting their money work for them with the intention and purpose of increasing their net worth. This can be you too!

Most associate investing in the stock market with high levels of risk and that only the people who are successful at it are villainous or cold-hearted speculators. And so they keep their money on deposit at the bank with less than 1% in annual interest. But you are different. You want more in life than exchanging your time for money in the form of a paycheck. You do not want to just go to work, collect a paycheck, buy a house with an expensive mortgage, pay taxes, and get further in debt than your income allows. You are not a sheep following the flock. You are different.You want financial independence. Yes, you are different. Different because you have a different mindset about investing in the stock market.

Because you are not just one of the flock and you stand out from those that would be sheep, you must also surround yourself with other people who standout and are experienced. These are the people pursuing economic independence through investment in the stock market. If you are surrounded by sheep, you will yourself become one. You must think like a successful person to be a successful person. Be different!

There are important skills an investor should possess. The following are entrepreneurial skills the benefit an investor.

- Take responsibility for your decisions, whether good or bad. Own your mistakes and celebrate your successes.

- Get out of your comfort zone. We are creatures of habit. We do what's easy. To break out of your habits and strive for making a difference, get out of your comfort zone.

- Have a back-up plan in case your investment fails. Dale Carnegie said "Develop success from failures. Discouragement and failures are two of the surest stepping stones to success." Knowing that failure is likely, especially in the beginning, give yourself a little cushion to soften the blow.

- Optimize your resources. Be your own MacGyver and use what you have.

- Be prepared for continuous learning.Investing is not a static skill. It's a path of continuous learning where thirst for knowledge equals success. The smartest entrepreneurs are constantly evolving andchanging their approach based on learnings and market feedback.

- Understand that time is treated differently when investing. Often you will be making decisions based on uncertainty. Short- and long-term goals require different approaches. What you do (or don't do) today will have an impact down the road. Imagine if you bought stock in Apple 30 years ago!

- It's about the numbers. Numbers are the indicators of your investment's success or failure. Pay attention to and learn to understand what the numbers are telling you. This means understanding a stock's prospectus and not just looking at its returns in the last 12 months.

- Trust your instincts. If it does not feel right, don't do it! But do not confuse trepidation with that feeling of excitement and newness. With some experience you will begin to tell the difference.

- Act. In the wise words of Lao Tzu, "A journey of a thousand miles must begin with a single step."

Emotional decisions are often regrettable and the same is true for making emotional investment decisions. Emotional decisions come in the form of fear of missing out on opportunity (eg. cryptocurrency) or fear of losing it all. These fears are fueled by social media and 24 hours news. We are living in world where major markets overlap in time zones and that combined with 24 hours news can lead to exaggerated and irrational investment behavior. So how to you handle this kind of environment and make sure you avoid being caught up in fervor of irrationality?

There are several methods you might employ in order to maintain your composure. Popular methods include diversification, staggering buy and sell decisions, choose dividend paying stocks, and limiting investments in volatile commodities, such as oil. Basically, focus on metrics, be objective and willing to change your investment strategy depending on your goals and market performance.

I will leave you with one last thought about mindset and why you are even thinking this way...

In the words of John Rampton, "Don't let money run your life, let money help you run your life better."

Chapter 1:

An Introduction to

Dividend Stocks

In this chapter, we are going to explain what a dividend stock is using an explanation designed for complete beginners. Our goal here is to make sure that everyone has a clear understanding of what dividend stocks are, how they differ from stocks that don't pay dividends and why, and how you make money from them. If you already have some idea of how this works, this chapter will function as a review. Let's get started!

Overview of the Stock Market

Most people don't direct their own retirement or investment accounts, so they may not have a complete understanding of what the stock market is and how it operates. Using a "set it and forget it" mentality, they have 401k plans, and possibly they invest in mutual funds. Both are passive investment vehicles from the perspective of the investor that are managed by someone else. As a result, a lot of people only pay vague attention to their retirement plans, and the actual workings of the stock market might be a little bit mysterious.

People simply accept what their 401k or the mutual fund gives them, and they really don't put much thought into it.

Our education here is going to be brief and far from complete, but let's start from the ground up. This begins with an investigation into what stock really is. In short, it's an ownership stake in a company.

A company that wants to grow will issue shares of ownership in the company. It doesn't have to be a publicly-traded company to do this. The company can decide how much it's worth. Usually, this will be based on its revenues over some past time period, but sometimes they will value themselves based on projected revenues. Then they will decide what percentage of the company to sell off, and issue shares of stock in the company, which is basically a slice of ownership.

Suppose that a small company is worth $100,000. In order to raise capital so the company can expand, the current owners decide to sell a 40% stake in the company. A small company might sell a minority stake so that the current owners can retain a majority stake in the business since selling stock gives owners voting rights in the company. They could sell that stake to one person for $40,000, or they could divide that up into 100 shares that cost $400 each. Shares of stock are issued with a certificate showing the ownership stake.

Investors could buy as little as one share in the company or as many as they can afford and are available. A private company can sell shares to friends, or venture capitalists that might be interested in the company, but they cannot sell shares to the general public. Private companies are not listed on an exchange where shares of stock are bought and sold.

Shares of stock in a company entitle those who own those shares to a share of company profits. Those will be paid out to owners on an agreed-upon basis. If the company's revenues go up, the value of the shares will increase since the holder of the stock will be entitled to receive a larger amount of money when profits are paid out to the owners. On the other hand, if the company falls on hard times, the shares won't be worth as much, because the owner will receive smaller payments.

If it's a private company, the owner of shares of stock might find it difficult to get out of the investment if they want to. They could sell the shares back to the company if they are willing to buy them back. Otherwise, they will have to find a buyer to accept the shares.

As companies get larger, they may decide to "go public." This means that they will be publicly traded on an exchange. You are probably familiar with some of the large exchanges where shares of stock are publicly traded, including the New York

Stock Exchange or NASDAQ. Dividend investors are going to be investing in publicly traded companies.

The U.S. Securities and Exchange Commission regulates publicly traded companies. Although there are some pretty large privately held companies, those traded on major stock exchanges tend to be larger and worth a lot more money. However, there is quite a variation in size, ranging from companies worth tens of millions of dollars to companies worth tens of billions and even hundreds of billions of dollars. Companies that are publicly traded must meet strict requirements since they are selling shares to the general public. Their financial statements must be made available to the public, and they must provide a prospectus. These documents will help investors decide whether or not they want to invest in a company and whether or not it's a good and safe investment.

Shares of stock in publicly traded companies are sold on the exchanges through companies that are called brokerages. They may also be available indirectly, through mutual funds and exchange-traded funds. We will talk more about that later, but in that case, the shares are purchased by an investment company and made a part of their fund. As an individual investor, you will buy and sell shares using a brokerage, who actually does the transactions on your behalf on one of the major exchanges where the stock is traded.

Common and Preferred Stock

When most people think of stock, it's a "common" stock that they are thinking about. A common stock gives you an ownership stake in the company, complete with voting rights. However, with common stock, you are last in line as a creditor if the company goes under. In most situations, of course, that is an unlikely scenario, but remember that companies like GM and Bear Sterns ran into major trouble.

Preferred stock doesn't confer voting rights, but it often pays a high dividend yield and moves you further up the line behind the creditors. Not all companies offer it, but when investing for dividend income, you may consider investing in preferred stock.

What Are Dividends?

Simply put, a dividend is a payment made by the company to its investors out of its profits. Typically, dividends are paid out on a quarterly basis. The company is not required to pay dividends, and it is not required to use all of its profits to pay dividends. The amounts paid in dividends vary quite a bit from company to company.

Most companies are seeking growth. Some are older and more established, and so they may not be seeking growth in an aggressive fashion. Another factor that is important is the industry that the company is involved in. Some companies are in highly competitive growth industries, such as the tech companies. Think of Facebook, Apple, or Amazon. Others are in slow-moving industries. Drug stores might be an example of this. There is still room for growth, but the growth is smaller and much slower than the kind of growth a mover and shaker like Amazon is experiencing. Generally speaking, younger companies are going to see more rapid and aggressive growth than older companies.

Companies that are in high growth industries or in a high growth phase are going to want to invest more of their profits back into the company. These profits are going to be used for research and development, or expansion. They may build new plants, purchase new equipment, or hire more people. Those companies that are aggressively seeking growth are not going to be paying dividends, generally speaking.

There are some exceptions. Apple has been a high-growth company over the past twenty years. It is not a particularly old company; it's about 43 years old. We might call it middle-aged. However, the company has been very aggressive in introducing new technology and services, literally creating and taking over many sectors within the high tech world. For a time, it was the most highly valued company in the world.

However, Apple is a company that pays dividends. Apple does engage in a lot of growth activity, including research and development. However, they pay out a fraction of their profits to investors in the form of dividends.

It's companions in the FAANG universe, which includes other high-tech giants like Facebook, Netflix, Amazon, and Google—don't pay dividends. These companies are reinvesting all of their profits into future growth. So they have no profits left over to pay out to investors.

Other industries are going to be characterized by dividend stocks. For example, utilities are not going to be high-growth stocks, but they are going to be reliably paying dividends.

Some industries are growing, but not at the rapid pace of the high-tech world. An excellent example of this is the healthcare and pharmaceutical sector. You are going to find many companies in this sector that pay good dividends, but the pharmaceutical industry is definitely growing, and these companies are going to be investing a lot of their profits back into research and development.

Here is the bottom line. When choosing companies to invest in, you will have to seek out companies that pay dividends, because many companies choose not to.

Dividend Yield and Annual Payout

When you begin searching for stocks to invest in, you are going to want to check the amount of the dividend payment and the yield. The dividend yield is the ratio of the dividend to the share price expressed as a percentage. You don't necessarily want to go for the highest yield stocks. Many stocks that have high yields are junk, stock issued by penny stock companies. These are not good investments for most people. They offer high yields in an effort to attract investors. However, you may be putting your capital at high risk by investing in such companies.

Instead, you want to focus either on well-known and established companies like Apple and IBM, or invest in index funds that pay dividends. If you are interested in higher yields, you may be able to find a suitable index or mutual fund for that purpose. That way, your risk is spread out rather than depending on one or two stocks that might pay high yields but be very high risk as far as your capital is concerned.

Another factor when selecting a dividend stock is longevity. We expect companies like Apple and IBM to be around for a long time, and they are likely to remain strong in the coming decades and possibly last well into your retirement. IBM is a hundred-year-old company, and although it's not as dominant as it once was, it remains stable, profitable, and reliable. These are the types of companies that you want to select for your dividends.

Let's take a closer look at how yields are calculated so that you understand what you are looking at when checking dividend payments for stocks. First of all, a listing for a stock will include the dividend payment. It's important to understand that this is the annual dividend payment. So if you look up some stock like ABC company and you see that its dividend payment is:

$8

That means each share pays $8 for the entire year. Dividends are paid out on a quarterly basis, so each quarter you would receive a payment of $8/4 = $2 since there are four quarters per year. If the shares are trading at $200 a share, then the yield, which is going to be expressed as a percentage, is going to be:

Dividend Yield = $8/$200 x 100 = 0.04 x 100 = 4%.

Let's check some real examples so that you can see how these numbers work out. First, let's go ahead and take a look at IBM since we've been talking about it so that you can see what they are actually paying. The quote will be listed as the forward dividend and yield. This means it's the expected payments in the future or going "forward."

For IBM, the dividend payment is listed as $6.48. Remember that this is the annual payment you can expect if you buy a share of IBM stock. So each quarter, you can expect to receive a payment of $1.62 per share.

To find the yield, we need the current share price. At the time of writing, IBM is trading at $140.75. So the yield is:

IBM Yield = $6.48/$140.75 x 100 = 0.046 x 100 = 4.6%

Since yield is given in terms of share price, it's constantly changing day to day and even throughout the day as the share price changes. This value may differ slightly from the forward dividend yield that is often quoted on stock sites, because they may be estimating future stock values rather than using the price per share that is quoted at the exact moment that you look up the stock. Of course, in some cases, that is hard to estimate.

Many companies are going to try and keep their yield constant or within a specified range. They do this in order to attract investors who like dividend stocks, because a stable yield is something that you can use to have a solid handle on your income from investments down the road, and you can compare it to other investment opportunities like savings accounts, money market funds, bank CDs, or bonds.

When you check a stock, something you can do is look at the past dividend history over time. One thing that you should check is how the company handles downturns in the economy, so looking at the dividend payments during the 2008 crash and the subsequent recession is going to be something that you will want to check. Companies that try and pay consistent dividends when times get tough are going to be better investments than companies that skimp on payments during recessions. After all, you don't want to be retired and suddenly have your income crash when there is a market downturn.

Another metric that you'll want to look at is the dividend payout ratio. This is given by the following formula:

Dividend Payout Ratio = (dividend paid per share)/(earnings per share) x 100

You probably won't have to do the calculation on some stock sites, but others may not provide it, but they will give the dividend payment per share and earnings per share. What this ratio does is it gives you an idea of how able the company is to pay the current yield. The first thing to observe here is that if this ratio is greater than 100%, that indicates that the company is paying out more than it's taking in. Obviously, this does not reflect well on the company's current circumstances, and chances are your dividend payments are going to be dropping in the coming months.

Believe it or not, there are many companies that pay dividends that are high enough to take the payout ratio well over 100%. In some cases, this means trouble ahead, and if the company's future prospects are not good, that can mean that you're going to see a huge cut in your dividend payments per share in the coming months or years.

However, this is not always the case. So you need to be careful when evaluating this metric. Sometimes companies are expecting higher earnings going forward. So you should not just be checking the current value of this metric or past dividend payments, but you should also be looking at the expectations of the company going forward. If a company is poised for strong earnings growth, that can mean that your dividend payments are actually secure, and will probably remain constant. In fact, they might even grow. So you will have to check the earnings outlook for a company before making a decision based on this metric so that you are not misled by the apparent value of the statistic. As we will see later, this is one reason why fundamental analysis is important for self-directed dividend investors. Fundamental analysis means checking the financial health of the company by going through its prospectus and financial statements in detail. We will cover this in the last chapter for those who are new to this type of activity.

There are several websites you can use to find out dividend information for publicly traded companies. Your own broker is probably going to have that information available, but two free resources you can use to find out basic information include Yahoo Finance and Dividend.com. The web links for both sites are listed below.

You can visit https://finance.yahoo.com to look up dividends for different stocks.

The main site used by dividend investors is https://dividend.com

Ex-Dividend Date and Date of Record

An important thing to be aware of besides the size of dividend payment and its yield is the date that dividends are actually paid out. The first thing to note is the record date. This is the date that the company will record who owns stock and who is entitled to a dividend payment. The ex-dividend date usually occurs one day before the record date. The company's board of directors will determine when these dates are. These dates can be important when it comes to buying and selling stocks. If you are buying stocks that pay dividends, you can make sure that you receive the payments by purchasing your shares well before the ex-dividend date, which is pretty much listed on most stock market sites when looking up the company of interest. When buying stock, you must purchase it by the ex-dividend date in order to receive the dividend payment. Otherwise, the seller will be the "owner of record" and would receive the dividend payment.

So just keep this rule in mind—purchase your shares on or before the ex-dividend date. Or wait for it to pass but don't expect your first dividend payment until the following quarter.

For most dividend investors, this is not a huge issue because you are more than likely going to be in your stock for the long-term. People who are actively trading stocks such as swing traders are going to be more concerned about making or missing these dates. They can also be important for options trading. But those approaches to the stock market are not the topic of this book. We are assuming that you are going to be a long-term investor and so looking to buy and hold stocks that pay good dividends.

If the record date falls on a Monday, the ex-dividend date will actually fall on the previous Thursday. This is something to keep in mind. Knowing that the ex-dividend date is normally one day before the date of the record, an investor could make a mistake of buying shares on Friday if the date fell on a Monday. In that case, they would be making a mistake if they were expecting to receive the dividend payment.

On all other days, if the date of the record falls on a Tuesday–Friday, then the ex-dividend date is one day prior.

Also, keep these dates in mind when selling shares. If you had been holding shares of stock for a long time, the last thing you want to do is sell them right before the ex-dividend date and miss out on your last dividend payment. You will want to sell them after the date of the record passes instead.

Although options trading is not a subject that is covered in this book, some long-term investors seek to earn extra income from selling covered calls against their shares. If you are doing this, you will also want to avoid selling covered calls around the ex-dividend date, which might increase the odds that your shares get called away if the option is in the money.

Dividends and Share Appreciation

There are two ways to gain wealth as a dividend investor. The first is through the dividend payments that you receive each quarter. These can be taken as cash payments or reinvested to purchase new shares of stock. If you are earlier in your investment career or getting started late, and so you need to acquire as many shares as possible, for now, its recommended that you reinvest the proceeds in order to purchase more shares. The more shares that you acquire, the larger your income from dividends is going to be in the future.

You will also acquire wealth through the normal appreciation of the shares that happens as time goes on. Although companies like Apple or IBM are paying dividends, with time, the value of their shares increases as well. Of course, we suppose that the companies remain stable and profitable.

When the value of the shares increases, you are going to increase your wealth. Also, if the company works to keep its yields consistent, your dividend payments may increase as well.

Summary

We have learned that some stocks pay dividends, and some stocks don't. The reason that stocks may not pay dividends is usually related to their growth prospects. Some aggressively growing companies are reinvesting all of their profits into growth, such as research and development, building new plants, or engaging in other activities geared toward rapid growth. Some companies, like Apple, pay dividends while still seeking aggressive growth. One reason they might do this is the dividend helps to attract investors. Finally, other companies are in a more stable phase and will pay steady dividends.

The key factors to look for are the dividend payment, yield, and payout ratio. You are going to be more interested in high yields, but be sure to balance that against the health of the company and its long-term prospects.

In the next chapter, we are going to investigate some of the benefits of dividend stocks. This will include an example of compound interest. You can think of dividend stocks as a kind of high growth savings account. The dividend payments are like interest, but unlike a bank account, your "principal," which is the cash tied up owning the shares of stock themselves, can grow as well making this a far more powerful investment. At any time down the road, you are always free to sell off shares of stock that have appreciated in value to take the profits.

We are also going to discuss how much you should plan on investing in order to get the kind of income that you want from dividends. For most people, this is going to be a long-term project, so you will accumulate the number of shares that you want over an extended time period. If you have enough cash on hand now, however, you will be able to invest right away and begin enjoying the dividend payments if you want to. We are also going to talk a bit about the tax implications. One thing that we will be looking at is the different tax rules you are likely to face when it comes to taking dividend payments and selling off stock for profits.

Chapter 2:

The Pros of Investing in Dividend Stocks

When people think of the stock market, they tend to think in terms of appreciation in the share price. The goal is to buy low and sell high, at some later date. Even methodical and long-term investors are often thinking in these terms, with the hope that they can wait until retirement and then cash out a small portion of their portfolio every year to generate income to live on. Generally speaking, people hope to have a stock portfolio worth a million dollars or more and cash out something like 4% of it each year.

Dividend investing can take advantage of that too, but the main goal with dividend investing is to purchase stocks that not only appreciate in value but also payout profits, usually on a quarterly basis. This enables you to hold onto your stock portfolio while it generates income that you can live on, year after year.

The amount of income you earn is obviously going to be proportional to the number of shares that you hold, but it's also going to depend on the yield as well. When the yield is higher, you aren't going to have to own as many shares. If you plan ahead, you can set yourself up to earn almost any level of income that you desire.

Unfortunately, financial literacy is not a strong point in today's America. As a result, many people are, in fact, not planning ahead. Since you have chosen to read this book, you are at least thinking about it, which is an important step. However, if you are later in life (investment-wise), meaning your 40s or 50s or even your 60s, while it is going to be possible to build up an income from dividend stocks, you are going to have to be far more aggressive in your approach. That means that you are probably going to have to cut back on your lifestyle now, in order to ensure that in the future, you will be better placed to have the number of shares that you need in order to enjoy a sustainable income.

Let Your Money Work For You With Compound Interest

The power of dividend investing as compared to simply buying stocks is that it takes advantage of compound interest. This is perhaps the most fundamental lesson that anyone should take away from finance. You can think of compound interest as having your money work for you, rather than the usual way it works, which is you working for money.

Compound interest works by earning interest on money that you invest. So if you put $1,000 in a savings account, the bank is going to pay you interest on that $1,000. If you put an additional $500 a year, your principal is growing with time. The first $1,000 that you put into the account is called your initial principal. However, the power of compound interest comes from the fact that previous interest payments—assuming that you are not pulling them out and blowing them on pizza and beer—add to the principal in your account. So each time interest is added to your principal, you have a larger amount of money that is going to earn interest in the next cycle. Thus, you are earning interest on the initial principal plus the interest that has been earned in previous periods. In other words, the interest is compounding. This sets up a situation where an amount of capital can grow rapidly. If you make sure that you are putting more money into the account each year, then you are going to make it grow even faster.

The idea was a concept that once made simply putting money in the bank a safe and worthwhile way of building up a nest egg to rely on in emergencies or the future. It has been that way for centuries, with roots going back at least into middle-aged Europe.

Unfortunately for people who are strict savers, the Federal Reserve (and other central banks around the world) has continually lowered interest rates. This has been their strategy to keep the economy juiced, but one side effect of this is that bank accounts pay virtually nothing these days. At best, they are keeping up with inflation, and in reality, some of the purchasing power of money kept in the bank is probably decreasing slowly with time. There doesn't seem to be any indication that this is going to change any time soon.

Another way that you can earn interest is by investing in bonds. A bond is basically a loan that you give to some institution. It can be government or corporate, and the U.S. government is one of the most famous entities that issue bonds. Most large corporations borrow money by issuing bonds to the public as well. When you invest in bonds, you are basically playing the role of the bank. The company or government agency that issues the bonds will pay you interest for your troubles.

However, like bank accounts, bonds are not as attractive as they once were. While you can find some higher interest rates on bonds (in particular when the issuing entity is not in good credit shape), generally speaking, the interest rates are low, historically speaking. At best, they are keeping up with inflation.

This leaves us with dividend stocks. Dividend stocks work by using compound interest. You can think of them as a savings account in these terms. Your initial principal would be the shares that you purchase in a given company. Unless you have a large amount of capital to invest right away, you are going to want to take your dividend payments and reinvest them, in order to accumulate more shares at a faster pace. This is equivalent to the interest payments in the bank that are added to the principal in your account. So the dividend payments act like interest, and you can check the yield to make a comparison. But unlike a bank account, the shares themselves are usually acquiring increased value as time goes on. So you may buy shares at $50 a share now, but in 5 years they might be trading at $100 a share or even more. So the amount of growth that you can see with dividend investing is going to be a lot larger than what you're going to see when it comes to a bank account or bond investing. When you buy bonds, your principal is the principal. It's not going to grow by itself. But with stocks that are appreciating in value, it's often as if the principal itself is growing. You are going to want to look at the history of a company that you are interested in investing in. Check to see if they increase their dividend payment as the company grows and its stock price appreciates. This indicates that the company is committed to paying a certain yield, and you can count on this company for solid dividend payments.

Of course, share prices are not always going to increase. Sometimes a company stagnates, or worse it begins performing at a lower level. But one advantage of the stock market is that this isn't necessarily a problem either. Each year, you can evaluate your portfolio and sell off stocks that are not performing and replace them with better stocks. So there is a bit of inherent flexibility that is not always available with other investments.

In order to understand the power of compound interest, it helps to use an example. So let's say that we are going to invest $100,000 and that the interest rate is 5%. Further, we'll assume that we are going to invest an additional $500 a month. After 30 years, we are going to have earned more than $584,000 in interest, and end up with an account with $864,637.62.

Year	Year Deposits	Year Interest	Total Deposits	Total Interest	Balance
1	$6,000.00	$5,281.20	$106,000.00	$5,281.20	$111,281.20
2	$6,000.00	$5,858.37	$112,000.00	$11,139.56	$123,139.56
3	$6,000.00	$6,465.06	$118,000.00	$17,604.63	$135,604.63
4	$6,000.00	$7,102.80	$124,000.00	$24,707.43	$148,707.43
5	$6,000.00	$7,773.16	$130,000.00	$32,480.59	$162,480.59
6	$6,000.00	$8,477.82	$136,000.00	$40,958.41	$176,958.41
7	$6,000.00	$9,218.54	$142,000.00	$50,176.95	$192,176.95
8	$6,000.00	$9,997.15	$148,000.00	$60,174.10	$208,174.10
9	$6,000.00	$10,815.59	$154,000.00	$70,989.69	$224,989.69
10	$6,000.00	$11,675.91	$160,000.00	$82,665.59	$242,665.59
11	$6,000.00	$12,580.24	$166,000.00	$95,245.84	$261,245.84
12	$6,000.00	$13,530.84	$172,000.00	$108,776.68	$280,776.68
13	$6,000.00	$14,530.08	$178,000.00	$123,306.75	$301,306.75
14	$6,000.00	$15,580.43	$184,000.00	$138,887.19	$322,887.19
15	$6,000.00	$16,684.53	$190,000.00	$155,571.72	$345,571.72
16	$6,000.00	$17,845.11	$196,000.00	$173,416.83	$369,416.83
17	$6,000.00	$19,065.07	$202,000.00	$192,481.91	$394,481.91
18	$6,000.00	$20,347.45	$208,000.00	$212,829.36	$420,829.36
19	$6,000.00	$21,695.44	$214,000.00	$234,524.79	$448,524.79
20	$6,000.00	$23,112.39	$220,000.00	$257,637.18	$477,637.18
21	$6,000.00	$24,601.83	$226,000.00	$282,239.02	$508,239.02
22	$6,000.00	$26,167.48	$232,000.00	$308,406.50	$540,406.50
23	$6,000.00	$27,813.23	$238,000.00	$336,219.73	$574,219.73
24	$6,000.00	$29,543.18	$244,000.00	$365,762.91	$609,762.91
25	$6,000.00	$31,361.64	$250,000.00	$397,124.54	$647,124.54
26	$6,000.00	$33,273.13	$256,000.00	$430,397.67	$686,397.67
27	$6,000.00	$35,282.42	$262,000.00	$465,680.09	$727,680.09
28	$6,000.00	$37,394.50	$268,000.00	$503,074.59	$771,074.59
29	$6,000.00	$39,614.65	$274,000.00	$542,689.24	$816,689.24
30	$6,000.00	$41,948.38	$280,000.00	$584,637.62	$864,637.62

What if instead, you put in $1,000 a month? In that case, you will cross the $800,000 mark by year 23, and in the end, you'll have a little more than $1.2 million.

Year	Year Deposits	Year Interest	Total Deposits	Total Interest	Balance
1	$12,000.00	$5,446.21	$112,000.00	$5,446.21	$117,446.21
2	$12,000.00	$6,338.79	$124,000.00	$11,785.00	$135,785.00
3	$12,000.00	$7,277.04	$136,000.00	$19,062.03	$155,062.03
4	$12,000.00	$8,263.29	$148,000.00	$27,325.32	$175,325.32
5	$12,000.00	$9,299.99	$160,000.00	$36,625.31	$196,625.31
6	$12,000.00	$10,389.74	$172,000.00	$47,015.05	$219,015.05
7	$12,000.00	$11,535.24	$184,000.00	$58,550.29	$242,550.29
8	$12,000.00	$12,739.35	$196,000.00	$71,289.64	$267,289.64
9	$12,000.00	$14,005.06	$208,000.00	$85,294.71	$293,294.71
10	$12,000.00	$15,335.53	$220,000.00	$100,630.24	$320,630.24
11	$12,000.00	$16,734.07	$232,000.00	$117,364.31	$349,364.31
12	$12,000.00	$18,204.16	$244,000.00	$135,568.47	$379,568.47
13	$12,000.00	$19,749.46	$256,000.00	$155,317.93	$411,317.93
14	$12,000.00	$21,373.82	$268,000.00	$176,691.75	$444,691.75
15	$12,000.00	$23,081.29	$280,000.00	$199,773.04	$479,773.04
16	$12,000.00	$24,876.12	$292,000.00	$224,649.16	$516,649.16
17	$12,000.00	$26,762.77	$304,000.00	$251,411.93	$555,411.93
18	$12,000.00	$28,745.95	$316,000.00	$280,157.87	$596,157.87
19	$12,000.00	$30,830.59	$328,000.00	$310,988.46	$638,988.46
20	$12,000.00	$33,021.88	$340,000.00	$344,010.34	$684,010.34
21	$12,000.00	$35,325.28	$352,000.00	$379,335.62	$731,335.62
22	$12,000.00	$37,746.54	$364,000.00	$417,082.16	$781,082.16
23	$12,000.00	$40,291.66	$376,000.00	$457,373.82	$833,373.82
24	$12,000.00	$42,967.00	$388,000.00	$500,340.82	$888,340.82
25	$12,000.00	$45,779.22	$400,000.00	$546,120.04	$946,120.04
26	$12,000.00	$48,735.31	$412,000.00	$594,855.36	$1,006,855.36
27	$12,000.00	$51,842.65	$424,000.00	$646,698.01	$1,070,698.01
28	$12,000.00	$55,108.96	$436,000.00	$701,806.97	$1,137,806.97
29	$12,000.00	$58,542.38	$448,000.00	$760,349.35	$1,208,349.35
30	$12,000.00	$62,151.46	$460,000.00	$822,500.81	$1,282,500.81

If you are coming to your investment program late, you can use compound interest calculators to get an estimate of how much extra you would need to put into your account each month in order to cross a given amount of money. Let's say that our goal is one million dollars. If we were over 50, getting to a million dollars would be tough. You might be able to do it by age 70 if you make a large monthly deposit, on the order of $2,000 or more. That means that you are going to have to live a frugal lifestyle in the meantime, or possibly get a second source of income that can be devoted entirely to investing. Of course, higher interest rates can help, too. One of the beauties of the stock market, is that unlike bank accounts, you can find much higher yields. That may entail higher levels of risk, but each 1 point differential you add to the yield can mean growing your account size much faster. For example, a 7% interest rate could get you to a million dollars in fifteen years, with monthly deposits of $2,500.

Now, keep in mind that dividend yield is calculated using the current share price, and that a healthy company is going to be wanting to keep its yield fairly constant. Second, keep in mind that share prices are growing with time. To see how this works, let's take a look at some of the history behind IBM.

IBM is trading at around $140 a share at the time I am writing this book. It's actually been higher than this, but in 1993 it was trading for $12 a share. Just to be sure—we can check an inflation calculator. Something that costs $12 in 1993 would cost $21 today. So the price of a share of IBM stock has far outstripped inflation. Even in 2006, it was only trading for $74 a share.

| 1 day | 5 days | 1 month | 6 months | YTD | 1 year | 5 years | **Max** |

In fact, in 1989, it was less than $4 a share. That is your 30 period of growth—going from $4 a share all the way up to $140 a share (in fact it was higher for a while). If the company is trying to be consistently paying dividends, then you will get the same yield with a higher dividend payment. In fact, over the past ten years or so, the quarterly payments made by IBM have increased from $0.50 a share to $1.62 per share.

What this illustrates is that with good, solid companies, the share price is going to grow over time. But I don't want to give you a completely rosy picture, because the real world is more complicated than that and I would be lying if I suggested every company you invest in is going to work out in this way. An example of a company that has stumbled is GE, which for many decades was taken to be a solid dividend stock. In 1993, GE was going for around $8 a share. It surged to $50 a share by the end of the decade. However, during the stock market crash in 2008, it plummeted to around $12 a share, and while it recovered some of its value to $30 a share during the Obama presidency, it has dropped since—down to $10 a share. So it's at the same level as it was in 1993. It has actually lost a little bit of value because using our inflation calculator we find that $8 in 1993 is worth $14 today.

These examples illustrate why diversification is an important part of any investment strategy. Some of the stocks that you invest in are going to work out, but not all of them are going to do so. That is why you should never put all of your investment dollars into one company. Certainly, in 1993, GE might have had that appeal, and some people probably did put everything they had into GE. They probably aren't very happy now. But if you use an effective strategy of diversification, you can avoid problems like these. You also have to be willing to get out of a stock when it is clear that it's not going to help you reach your goals. We will be talking about some of these issues in more detail in chapter 4 of this book.

The Power of Share Appreciation with Yield to Give Higher Compound Interest

If you have a good stock, you can think of the total value of your portfolio in terms of an interest rate that would be calculated by adding the yield for the dividend payment to the annual growth rate in the share price. For our purposes right now, we are going to assume that you reinvest all of your dividend payments during the growth phase for your portfolio. So you will have to take into account the returns from your dividend yields, plus the return on the shares of stock themselves. That is a little bit more complicated, and we aren't going to get into the details because this is not a financial mathematics book, but rather than looking at a return of 3-5%, you are going to be looking at higher returns that could range anywhere from 6-11% depending on the specifics of the stock we are looking at. Some ETFs have very strong growth rates; in good times, you can even find annual returns in excess of 10%. But those that pay dividends are probably going to have lower yields on the order of 2%.

But just for an example, let's consider an initial investment of $25,000 with a total rate of return of 8%. We will set monthly contributions to $1,000. The results are pretty amazing. Over a 30 year period, you can end up with a total of $1.7 million.

Year	Year Deposits	Year Interest	Total Deposits	Total Interest	Balance
1	$12,000.00	$2,607.91	$37,000.00	$2,607.91	$39,607.91
2	$12,000.00	$3,820.36	$49,000.00	$6,428.28	$55,428.28
3	$12,000.00	$5,133.45	$61,000.00	$11,561.72	$72,561.72
4	$12,000.00	$6,555.51	$73,000.00	$18,117.23	$91,117.23
5	$12,000.00	$8,095.61	$85,000.00	$26,212.84	$111,212.84
6	$12,000.00	$9,763.54	$97,000.00	$35,976.38	$132,976.38
7	$12,000.00	$11,569.90	$109,000.00	$47,546.28	$156,546.28
8	$12,000.00	$13,526.19	$121,000.00	$61,072.47	$182,072.47
9	$12,000.00	$15,644.85	$133,000.00	$76,717.32	$209,717.32
10	$12,000.00	$17,939.36	$145,000.00	$94,656.68	$239,656.68
11	$12,000.00	$20,424.31	$157,000.00	$115,080.99	$272,080.99
12	$12,000.00	$23,115.51	$169,000.00	$138,196.51	$307,196.51
13	$12,000.00	$26,030.08	$181,000.00	$164,226.59	$345,226.59
14	$12,000.00	$29,186.56	$193,000.00	$193,413.15	$386,413.15
15	$12,000.00	$32,605.03	$205,000.00	$226,018.18	$431,018.18
16	$12,000.00	$36,307.22	$217,000.00	$262,325.40	$479,325.40
17	$12,000.00	$40,316.70	$229,000.00	$302,642.10	$531,642.10
18	$12,000.00	$44,658.96	$241,000.00	$347,301.06	$588,301.06
19	$12,000.00	$49,361.62	$253,000.00	$396,662.68	$649,662.68
20	$12,000.00	$54,454.61	$265,000.00	$451,117.29	$716,117.29
21	$12,000.00	$59,970.31	$277,000.00	$511,087.59	$788,087.59
22	$12,000.00	$65,943.81	$289,000.00	$577,031.40	$866,031.40
23	$12,000.00	$72,413.10	$301,000.00	$649,444.51	$950,444.51
24	$12,000.00	$79,419.35	$313,000.00	$728,863.86	$1,041,863.86
25	$12,000.00	$87,007.11	$325,000.00	$815,870.97	$1,140,870.97
26	$12,000.00	$95,224.65	$337,000.00	$911,095.62	$1,248,095.62
27	$12,000.00	$104,124.25	$349,000.00	$1,015,219.87	$1,364,219.87
28	$12,000.00	$113,762.50	$361,000.00	$1,128,982.37	$1,489,982.37
29	$12,000.00	$124,200.73	$373,000.00	$1,253,183.10	$1,626,183.10
30	$12,000.00	$135,505.32	$385,000.00	$1,388,688.42	$1,773,688.42

These examples are for illustration only. Keep in mind that actual results are going to be different and these don't represent real investments. However, they do illustrate the concept quite nicely. If you pick a good stock with growth potential and reinvest your dividends, then by the time you retire you are going to have a far larger fund to draw on than you would from virtually any other type of investment.

Grow Faster with DRIPS (Dividend Reinvestment Plans)

When you start researching dividend-paying stocks, a term that you are going to start seeing is DRIP. What on earth does that mean?

A DRIP is a Dividend-Re-Investment-Plan. If you are not ready to start taking income from your portfolio and you are hoping to grow it with time, you should use DRIPs when this is available. You will have to look at the actual stocks you select to invest in and also check with your brokerage for specifics.

The advantage of this type of plan is that your dividend payments will be automatically reinvested. So if you have shares of Exxon, if you have it set up in this way, then your dividend payments from Exxon will be used to purchase additional shares of Exxon each quarter. This is the best way to set up your investment portfolio so that you will have the best possible scenario waiting for you when you get close to retirement and start taking out the dividend payments for income. It's going to help you grow your investments faster than would otherwise be possible because you will be automatically adding even more shares per quarter.

One of the nice things about DRIPS is that you can even purchase fractional shares in many cases. That way, not a penny of your dividend payments is wasted. A fractional share may not sound like much but think about adding up shares over the course of five, ten, 15, or 20 years. Just like anything else, it will add up and put you in a much better and more secure position down the road.

When you are ready to start taking income from your dividend payments, then you can simply work with your broker to readjust your settings so that instead of the further purchase of shares, you start getting cash payments in your account. Then you can take them out and use them to fund your living expenses.

How Much to Invest to Generate The Passive Income You Need

You should not go about investing without a plan. In the case of dividend investing, you are going to need to have an idea of how much income you want to get from your dividend stocks when you decide to start taking income. Some readers may find they have enough money now to buy the required number of shares, but most people are probably going to need to invest over the long term to get to where they want to go.

It is not going to be possible to be entirely accurate because there are many unknowns when it comes to predicting the future. For example, we cannot be sure what the inflation rate is going to be. So if you think that you need $40,000 in income now, you aren't going to be able to predict with certainty what $40,000 is going to look like in 10 or 20 years. One word of caution I would advise is noting that the government has high levels of debt, and this might lead to an inflation crisis at some point. I am not saying that it is going to, but it is possible. Consider that during the Carter years, inflation was something like 14%. So you can't be sure that the low rates of inflation we've enjoyed over the last 30 years are going to continue. We also can't be sure that the stock market will grow in the future in the same way that it did the past 50 years. There are so many uncertainties over long time periods you really don't know what is going to happen with complete certainty.

That said, you are going to have to make some assumptions. As the years go by, you can readjust your plan as necessary, which might mean that you have to make more sacrifices to keep heading where you want to go, or you might have to invest in stocks with more aggressive growth rates.

A starting point, at least to get an idea of where you are going, is to look at the number of shares you would need today in order to get the level of income that you desire. There are going to be many different factors to consider. But let's go ahead and start by looking at IBM once again. The current dividend payment is $6.28 per share. Remember that this is an annual payment.

Doing simple math, we find that in order to make $40,000 a year from IBM, we are going to need to own 6,370 shares of stock in IBM. This would require a total investment of $891,800 using an approximate share price of $140 a share, which is close to today's value. That is a yield of around 4.5%.

The point of this exercise is to show that in order to earn a decent amount of money, you are going to have to buy a large number of shares, and it's going to cost you. But that shouldn't be a point that keeps you from moving ahead with an investment plan, because to earn $40,000 per year from any investment, you are definitely going to have to come up with a lot of capital in order to do it. If you have a million dollars in your investment accounts right now, you can buy and sell shares in order to get the dividend-paying stocks that you want. If you don't have this amount of money available, then you are going to have to do what everyone else does, and that is, invest and grow your portfolio over time.

There are many options to consider. We have only been using IBM as an example. Later we will be talking about exchange-traded funds. One of these funds that you might be interested in is the stock ticker VYM. This is the Vanguard High Dividend Yield Fund. It has a yield of around 3%, and its $84 a share. It has an astounding year to date return of 13%.

Or consider BAP, which is Credicorp LTD. The share price is $209, but it pays a $20 dividend. So you won't need nearly as many shares, and you can get a good income with a smaller investment.

In this book you are only getting your feet wet, so if you are serious about becoming a dividend investor, you are going to have to do a lot of research in order to find out what the best stocks are for you to invest in so that you can meet your goals over the desired time frame.

A Mixed Portfolio

Don't think that when you look at all the possibilities for investment that things have to be strictly one way or the other. You can do whatever you want, but of course, if you want to earn a substantial dividend income down the road, you are going to have to accumulate a significant number of shares in dividend-paying stocks. That said, many investors also like to see some growth in their portfolio. So it's certainly permissible to purchase shares in high-growth stocks that are not paying dividends. At a later date, these shares can be sold for a profit, or you can even use the funds to buy more dividend-paying stocks, to ensure that you are setting up more income payments when you are heading into your retirement.

Many investors also put money on other instruments, such as bonds. So it is possible to divide up your portfolio to get extra diversity and to meet whatever goals you set for yourself.

However, you should not take a haphazard approach to investing. If you are hoping to get significant income from dividend stocks, this is going to require a significant portion of your investments. You should not be making decisions based on emotions when it comes to investing, so if you get excited over something that you want to invest in, you are going to have to remain disciplined so that you don't raid your income-producing assets.

In all cases, have a plan and stick to the plan. The more time that you have in order to invest, the more flexible your plan can be. Without a large amount of discretionary income, it is going to be difficult in order to come up with the necessary amount of money in order to build up a dividend income portfolio that gives you a significant income over a short time period. So if you have ten years or less left in your investment life, plan on getting very aggressive with your investing.

But investing without any kind of plan is certainly going to lead to shaky results. You need to know where you are going before you get started and stick to the plan, no matter what happens. Not being able to stick to a plan is one of the top mistakes that amateur investors make when trying to self-direct their accounts. All too often, amateur investors are easily drawn in by the excitement and other emotions that are often generated when investing, and seeing new opportunities that arise.

Chapter 3:
Dividend Income and Taxes

Understanding dividend income when it comes to taxation is going to be important when you are taking the money out as profit. Of course, if you are planning on taking the income out 10 or more years from now, it's impossible to know what kinds of changes Congress will implement in the meantime that could change what we say here. But with that in mind, let's briefly investigate what the current laws are.

Qualified vs. Non-Qualified Dividends

Dividend payments that you receive can be qualified or non-qualified. In part, this is determined by the type of entity that pays the dividends. While you might think this isn't going to matter in your situation, later in the book we are going to investigate some different types of dividends that are definitely of interest to investors, that will be treated differently for tax purposes.

A "qualified" dividend is a dividend that is paid out by a U.S. corporation. So if you are receiving dividend payments from a publicly traded corporation on the stock exchange, such as Apple, Facebook, or United Healthcare, this is a qualified dividend. However, you will have to check with your accountant in some circumstances because there are publicly traded companies on the major stock exchanges that pay dividends that are not qualified.

Foreign corporations are a special case, but they can be "qualified" if they are doing business in the U.S. and have a tax agreement in place with the United States.

But being paid by a corporation is not enough for the dividend to be qualified. The investor must hold the investment for 60 days or longer in order for it to be a qualified dividend payment. Otherwise, it is non-qualified, and as we will see in a moment that is an important distinction.

Furthermore, if the dividend is paid on preferred stock, the investment must have been held 90 days or more before the payment was made, to be considered as qualified.

Non-qualified dividends can come from several sources. These include real estate investment trusts, master limited partnerships, tax-exempt companies, mutual insurance companies, money market accounts, and employee stock options. So if you are receiving dividends from a company you work for as part of an employee stock option plan, those are non-qualified dividends.

How Are Qualified Dividends Taxed?

Qualified dividends are taxed as capital gains. The exact treatment is going to depend on how long you've held the investment. If you have held the stock for less than a year, qualified dividends are considered short-term capital gains. This means that they are going to be taxed as ordinary income tax rates.

However, once the asset has been held for a year or longer, qualified dividends are taxed as long-term capital gains. This means that dividend investors will get very favorable treatment for their dividend income payments. The exact tax rate will depend on the tax bracket determined by your ordinary income. For a single filer, the lowest long-term bracket is up to $38,600 in ordinary income, while for married couples filing jointly, the top income is $77,200. In this bracket, the tax rate for long-term capital gains is 0%.

The middle bracket goes from $38,601 up to $425,800 for single filers, and $77,201 to $479,000 for married couples filing jointly. The long-term capital gains tax rate, in this case, is 15%. For incomes above these levels, the capital gains tax rate is 20%. There is a Medicare surcharge tax of 3.8% that is added to the top bracket tax rate. It's not clear at the time of writing what the fate of this tax is going to be.

Tax Laws for Non-Qualified Dividends

When it comes to non-qualified dividends, they are taxed as ordinary income. However, we will need to investigate this issue further when it comes to certain entities such as master limited partnerships later in the book, so don't take the ordinary income label too far yet.

But generally speaking, income from non-qualified dividends is just going to be ordinary income taxed at your income tax rate. In addition, you may have to pay social security and Medicare taxes on this income. This book is not a tax advice book, and you should not consider any advice that we give here as actual tax advice without speaking to an accountant or licensed tax advisor, but the best approach is to pay some quarterly taxes out of your dividend proceeds when you receive your payments. A good rule of thumb is to pay in about 20-25% of it to the IRS as estimated depending on your tax bracket.

Of course, the specific rates and so forth are going to depend on your total level of income, and so it's impossible to give general tax advice in a book like this. But paying estimated taxes will save you a lot of trouble later on. So when setting your income goals, you will need to take taxation into account, and only consider about 75% or so of the dividend payments as the amount of income that you are going to be receiving if these dividends come from a non-qualified source. But again, you will need to be aware of the specific laws for special cases that we will be discussing later in the book.

When it comes to selling off shares of stock, if you have held them for less than a year, any profit that you make from selling the shares is considered short-term capital gains. If you hold your shares over the long-term, which in this case means one year plus one day or longer, then any profits that you make selling the shares will be considered long-term capital gains. These are looked on favorably by current law and are taxed as capital gains, at the lower capital gains tax rates. So later on in your investment career, you can always have the option of selling off shares of stock in order to raise cash.

Chapter 4:
Fundamental Analysis

As an individually directed investor, you are not going to be able to rely on the opinions of a financial manager. This means that you are going to have to investigate companies yourself and make your own determinations as to the financial health and prospects of the company. As we will see, diversification of your portfolio is going to be an important strategy to employ because your evaluations are going to be wrong in some cases, and secondly, companies have a habit of going bad down the road sometimes even though they look healthy now. The marketplace is dynamic, and changing factors and competition can always work against even the best companies.

As an investor, the important thing for you is not only to do a solid analysis of each company you invest in. You also need to keep up with the companies that you pick. That way, you can decide early on, long before the stock has a major collapse, whether or not to get out of the investment. Don't become wedded to a specific company. One of the mistakes that some self-directed investors make is they become too attached to a given company, falling in love with it and their dreams of getting a stream of dividend payments. But you should leave emotion out of it no matter how dedicated you feel you are to a given corporation. As much as possible, use pure logic to determine whether or not a given investment is a good one. And remember that things always change. Apple looked superb in 2011, now it's becoming questionable and not viewed as the innovative leader it once was. It might stay strong, but it could be on a long track of slow decline.

Remember that none of us has a crystal ball, and sometimes mistakes are going to be made. So there are going to be times when you decide to stick with a company, and it goes bust, and there are also going to be times when you decide to get out of an investment, and it turns out to be a bad decision because the company is able to turn itself around.

If you are careful and make good choices, this should only impact a small proportion of your investments. And if you have a few misses, don't beat yourself up over it. This even happens to professional financial managers. The key is to have more "wins" than "losses." If you are careful and methodical, it's not too difficult to build up a solid income-producing dividend portfolio.

What is Fundamental Analysis?

Fundamental analysis is an activity that looks at the company that is behind the stock you are thinking of investing in. In particular, we are interested in determining the financial health of the company, and its prospects going forward. Sometimes the value of the company is not going to be reflected in its current financial status. It could be based on the possession of groundbreaking technology. Tesla is a company that could fit the bill, although it seems to have a lot of management problems at the present time. Tesla does not pay dividends, and it's been losing money, but this is a good company to illustrate some outliers that you might keep an eye on or even invest in. Although the company has problems, it's also got a very innovative product that is poised to have a central position in the future. This illustrates that sometimes there are going to be different companies in different conditions that might be worth investing in—but of course, remember that they may carry risk. As of now, we don't know how Tesla is going to turn out, but the company does have value because of the products it has developed.

But for the most part, as a dividend investor, you should be focusing on companies that have long term stability and financial health. A good example is a company called Abbvie, which is a favorite among dividend investors. Abbvie is a pharmaceutical company. If you look it up, you are going to see it was founded in 2013, but it's actually a spin-off from Abbott Laboratories. So in truth, it's actually been in operation since 1888. Abbott Laboratories has actually changed focus, and Abbvie is actually carrying on the original activities of the company. It pays an annual dividend of $4.28 per share, with a yield of 6.5%, which is quite good.

That is more along the lines of the type of companies that you are going to be looking for when seeking dividend investments. However, you should be looking to build a diverse portfolio with a good mixture, across moderate risk to higher risk companies, spanning multiple sectors and company ages.

Types of Statements You Should Look At

The health of the company can be investigated using their financial statements, which are publicly available. The Securities and Exchange Commission requires that publicly traded companies make several documents available to the general public. A prospectus is one of these documents. This document is not only available for individual corporations; they are also available for mutual funds and exchange traded funds. These funds also pay dividends in many cases, and so they will also be of interest to some dividend investors.

The main documents you can examine include the Prospectus, 10K, Income Statement, Balance Sheet, and Cash Flow.

Prospectus

The prospectus will contain a lot of relevant information about the company. You will find information about the company's history and its management team. You can also find basic information about the kind of stock that it is offering and other securities such as bonds that are issued when a company takes on debt from the public.

If the prospectus is for a mutual fund, it will include information about the fund itself. This will include a description of the goals of the fund, such as whether it's the main goal is for income generation, rapid growth, or value stocks, for example. It will include information on dividend payments and yields, along with fees and costs associated with the fund and information on the fund's professional manager.

10K

Each year, a publicly-traded company must file an annual report with the Securities and Exchange Commission called the 10-K. The 10-K will contain thorough information about the company and its current status. You will find all of the financial statements associated with the company contained in it, along with information about the company itself.

Some of the information that is contained in the prospectus will also be included in the 10-K. The 10-K report contains all the basic information about the company, including its history and management team. You will also be able to find out the compensation packages paid to the management team, and other important information such as the structure of the company, the securities offered by the company, any subsidiaries it has, and audited financial statements. The three types of financial statements that you will want to look at are described below.

A 10-K report will also include information about the company's target market, and who they have identified as their competition.

Key Points for Financial Statements

Different types of financial statements convey different types of information. The first thing that you are going to look for is the profitability of the company. This is found in the company's income statement. Second, you will want to look at the company's net worth. To get this information, look at the balance sheet.

Some basic information, such as price to earnings ratio are also important. Compare the price to earnings ratio of the company to comparable companies in the same sector. If it is unusually high, this might be an overpriced stock that is due for a correction. On the other hand, if it's comparably low, you might have discovered a value stock that is available at a discount price. However, don't blindly look at the number and make your decisions based on this alone. A stock might have a high price to earnings ratio for other reasons—for example, it might be in possession of or developing a disruptive technology, that is probably going to increase the earnings of the company in the future. This is why a thorough analysis of a company is necessary before making a large investment.

As a dividend investor, you are going to be interested in determining the ability of the company to continue paying dividends. Obviously, we are limited in how far of an outlook we can have. The business environment is extremely volatile and constantly changing, so at the most, a five-year outlook is the best we can hope for, and even over the course of five years, many things can happen.

How to Read Financial Statements

Simply looking at a financial statement and then drawing conclusions from it isn't the only thing that you need to do. You also have to look at how the company is trending. So, for example, let's consider debt and liabilities. If a company has taken on a lot of debt, this could cause problems for dividend payments because the company is going to be obligated to make interest payments, but it is not obligated to make dividend payments of a certain size or even to make dividend payments at all. But while the absolute size of the debt is important, you should also look at how the debt is trending. If the company is reducing its debt load, this is actually a good sign going forward. On the other hand, if the company is increasing its debt load, that is not a good sign. If the debt is increasing, compare the rate of increase in debt to the rate of increase of other factors. For example, if the amount of debt the company is taking on is increasing, but earnings are increasing at a faster rate than debt, then the debt isn't necessarily a bad thing, at least for now. The debt may be helping the company expand and engage in more R & D.

The same holds for other financial information. And don't go in blindly no matter what you are looking at. For example, a company might show decreasing profits over recent quarters, but that could be because they are spending more on research and development in the near term. A technology or pharmaceutical company could be setting itself for higher profits down the road if that is the case. Everything needs to be evaluated in context.

Evaluating Net Worth

Stock market experts like to see a company that has an increasing net worth with time. You are going to want to look at the year-over-year comparisons of the net worth of companies that you are interested in investing in. Generally, the rule is that a healthy company is going to see an increasing net worth that is about 5-10% higher each year. Anything above this is certainly indicating that it's a very good investment.

Income Statements

Look at the income statements to review earnings, sales, expenses, and profits. You are going to want to check each item and compare it to the previous year's comparable quarter and probably go back five years when doing this. Profit is going to be important for dividends since dividends are paid out of profits. So you are going to want to see that profits are at the very least, staying steady. If they are increasing, that is even better. As dividend investors, we are hoping to find companies that are able to increase the level of their dividend payments over time. Also, pay attention to earnings per share.

Remember to check the payout ratio of the company, and see how it's progressing with time. This is the annual dividend per share, divided by the earnings per share. If the payout ratio is decreasing, that is a red flag. But you should determine the reasons it is decreasing before drawing conclusions.

Annual Report to the Shareholders

Another document that you should read is the annual report to the shareholders, including the letter from the chairman of the board. This will give you information on what the company thinks about its current situation and where it sees itself going forward. Some important things to pay attention to are any references to changing market conditions and developments in the industry. You should also carefully read this document to see how the company is addressing the challenges that it is facing. You can also find a letter from the accounting firm that is handling the company's financial statements. This is called the CPA opinion letter. This letter might have important information about the financial statements of the company.

Evaluations of the Company

After reviewing the prospectus, 10-K, financial statements, and annual report to the shareholders yourself, you may want to get more information on what professionals think about the company. You can do this by looking at reports about the company and buy, hold, or sell recommendations by financial analysts. Don't base your decisions on momentary news that is flying by on CNBC or other financial news sites that are based on hype and ratings. A dividend investor is interested in the long-term prospects of their investments, not short term fluctuations or even quarterly ups and downs. However, you will want to read analyst reports about different companies. Consider subscribing to a service like MorningStar, or Moody's Investment Service. These are going to help you form an opinion, but you should take them with a small grain of salt and utilize the information they provide in conjunction with what you have determined through your own analysis. The 2008 financial crisis showed that sometimes the worthiness of different investments as recommended by various experts and organizations (including Moody's) are not necessarily reliable.

Consider that Tesla is a company that is losing money, and it's rated as "overvalued." But many analysts are recommending it as a stock that you should buy.

Don't Invest in Gut Feelings

No matter what you do, you should not make large investments based on gut feelings. Emotion should not have a place in your investment decisions. Of course, this is an ideal situation. We are all human, and it's going to be impossible to eliminate emotion from our decisions completely. And sometimes, your emotions might even prove to be correct. In many cases, you can look at a new product that a company is putting out, and it will just feel right. And it will turn out to be a good "hunch." So we can't say that you should completely avoid making emotional decisions, but try keeping them to a minimum.

Do You Have to Be an Accountant?

The straightforward answer to this question is no. You do not have to be an accountant or have professional financial training to evaluate the financial health of a company. If you find that you don't understand what you are seeing in the financial statements, you can find assistance online that will explain what all the terms mean.

When it comes down to it, when you are evaluating the financial health of a corporation, it's not really any different from looking at the financial status of a household. You are simply looking at how much money is coming in, how much debt there is, and how much money is left over after paying expenses.

Chapter 5:

Beginning Your Investment Plan

We are going to cover investment planning over two chapters. In the next chapter, we are going to talk about strategies. These are methods that are used in order to implement your plan, but they are not really part of the plan itself. In this chapter, we are going to cover the process of getting set up in order to start your investing. So we will include picking a broker, buying stocks, and setting and meeting your investment goals.

Finding a Brokerage

These days, unless you are a day trader or something and doing a lot of frequent trading, finding a brokerage is actually quite easy. There are a couple of issues to consider, and these will include commissions and longevity. For starters, you are going to want to make sure that you are dealing with a legitimate brokerage firm. This is a highly regulated area of business, and so this really isn't an issue you have to worry too much about. The main thing that you might make sure you consider is don't invest with an overseas brokerage. Not very many people are going to fall into that trap, however, because as we noted this is a highly regulated business, and so they are going to have to notify you that they are not based in the United States.

Investing overseas will carry special risks that are beyond the scope of this book, but generally speaking, that is not something that you should be considering.

A good rule of thumb is to stick to well-known names. If you do that, you are probably going to get all your needs met without too much stress or expense. Among brokerages based inside the United States, the main issues that you might face include a minimum deposit to open an account and start trading, commissions, and length of time in business.

You'll also want to consider the range of tools that the broker has available. Since dividend investing is not something that involves staring at stock market charts all day long, hoping to see a tiny move in prices, you aren't really not going to have to worry about those kinds of assets. In fact, you can get most of the information that you need in order to be a dividend investor for free online. The main things that you are going to need is an ability to chart and look at past dividend payments. You will also want to be able to get the financial statements of the company and read their prospectus. However, all of this information is available for free. You can use Yahoo! Finance to look at stock charts and look at some of the information provided in financial statements. This information can also be obtained directly from the company.

What this boils down to is that you are not going to have to choose a broker that has a fancy setup, in the way a day or swing trader would. So this removes the tools part of the equation from the deal, unless that is really something that you are interested in having. For those who are only going to be using dividend investing as part of their overall investment plan, and you are also going to be doing some kind of trading with your account, then you might still be interested in seeking out a broker that offers a full suite of tools. The good news is that many of them do offer quite a few tools on their websites.

Of course these days something that you might be interested in is making sure that your broker is available across a wide range of technical platforms. So you probably want to avoid a broker that is only available through a website, you might want to be able to check stock prices and buy or sell shares using a mobile platform. So check the app store that you are using for your device, and you can use that to narrow down your choices.

Some brokerages will have a $0 minimum deposit, but of course, you are not going to be able to buy any stock under those conditions. But this allows you to start off by depositing an amount that you are comfortable with. Getting started by buying just a share or two a month is better than not investing at all, and as you are able, you can always increase your monthly contributions at a later date.

Some of the more popular brokerages include Charles Schwab, Fidelity, Ally Invest, Merryl Edge, Robinhood, E*Trade, Interactive Brokers, TD Ameritrade, and Trade Station. Some, like Robinhood, offer completely commission-free trades. Others require a $5-7 commission per trade, but in recent years there has been a move toward offering commission-free trades at least on some exchange-traded funds. For example, Charles Schwab offers commission-free trades on 503 exchange-traded funds, while Ally Invest offers commission-free trades on 116 of them.

When it comes down to it, you will just have to go with a broker that suits your needs. If you were a day trader, then the commissions would be a more important consideration. They might still be an important consideration, and the fact that many brokers like Robinhood are totally commission-free is an argument in their favor. However, with dividend investing, you are not going to be trading that frequently, so a few commissions might not be a huge deal.

How to Buy Stocks

Once you have opened an account, you need to deposit an adequate amount of money to buy shares. This process can happen pretty quickly in most cases, but it will vary from broker to broker. Be sure to deposit an adequate amount of money in order to get started. If you have a significant sum to invest, that doesn't mean that you should invest it all in a single day. You might want to take your time getting started and avoid rushing things. But if you have a clear idea of what stocks to buy to get started, and you plan to invest on a regular basis, you can go ahead and start buying stocks.

Buying and selling stocks is quite simple, especially if you are not "Trading." By trading, we mean that you are making short term stock purchases for the purpose of earning quick money. People who do this are called "day traders" if they hope to sell the stock the same day that they buy it, and they are called swing traders if they hope to sell the stock days or weeks later. These types of traders are interested in complex order schemes called stop loss and take profit orders, but as a dividend investor, these are not going to be of interest to you. You have multiple ways that you can place an order. For example, you can do a limit order or a market order. A limit order is an order that is placed to buy a stock at a specific price. It can be set to last until the end of the trading day or "good until canceled." Limit orders might not be filled because they won't execute unless the stock prices change so that it meets the limit price.

These kinds of pricing details, where someone is looking to make $1 or $5 off a share of stock, are not of interest to long-term investors, which means that dividend investors are probably not going to be concerned with such details.

What you should do as a dividend investor is simply place a market order. This is the default way of buying and selling a stock, and it will do the transaction at the market price or "mark," as it is sometimes called. It is going to fill the order at the market price that exists when someone actually decides to buy your shares or sell your shares. Remember that while we are using a computer to carry out the transaction, a real buyer or seller is on the other end of the deal. In most cases, market orders are filled pretty quickly. You might have to watch out a little when there is a rapidly declining or increasing share price. If your order is not getting filled and the share price is rapidly changing, then you can go ahead and place a limit order at that time in order to get it filled. If you are selling, then put the bid price for the limit. If you are buying shares, put the asking price.

This will help the order get filled quickly. Remember that as a dividend investor, you are probably going to be holding your shares for ten, twenty, or even thirty years. So a few cents or dollars one way or the other is not going to make a difference in your investment portfolio. Those kinds of expenses might matter to traders, but years from now the stock is going to be worth much more than it is now and any slight variations in the price are not going to be important.

There are different ways that you can go about buying your stock. You can buy your shares on a specific day of the month, or spread out your purchases. Again, 10 or 20 years from now, it's not going to matter very much. Many people like to buy on a specific day of the month, one so that they can keep disciplined and get in the habit of buying on a regular basis, and two it sets up a situation where they don't have to be thinking about their stocks very much. Of course, everyone is different, and you might want to keep a closer eye on your stocks than other people. In the end, however, it's not really going to matter all that much.

Placing an order is quite simple, although the details of the user interface will vary depending on the specific broker you use. There will be a "buy" or "sell" button that you click online or tap on your mobile phone. Then you will specify the number of shares that you want to purchase. If you don't have enough funds in your account, it will ask you to deposit funds. With many brokers, you can request a money transfer, and your account will be given instant credit so that you can go ahead with the stock purchase.

Margin Accounts and Day Trade Limitations

A day trade occurs if you buy and sell the same security during the same trading day. If you do four of these trades within five business days, you are going to be labeled a pattern day trader. If this happens, you either have to deposit $25,000 in your account, or it may be suspended or closed.

As a dividend investor, there is no reason to engage in any day trades. If you purchase any shares that you decide later that you don't want to keep, simply wait until the following day to sell them.

Likewise, you should not be using a margin account as a dividend investor. The purpose of a margin account is to borrow money or shares from the brokerage. You should not be borrowing in order to build up a dividend investing portfolio. The purpose of a margin account is to allow short-term traders to borrow so they can buy and sell more shares in a given trade. A margin account serves no purpose for dividend investing.

Setting Income Goals and Realizing Them

A good rule of thumb for a successful dividend investing portfolio is to figure on growing it to $500,000 up to a million dollars in stock. Of course, quite a bit of that is going to come from appreciation in share value over time. So instead of focusing on a dollar amount, it is better to set a goal focusing on the number of shares to acquire in order to earn a decent level of dividend income. A good rule of thumb is to shoot for 5,000–10,000 shares. If you can buy more, great, you should do so. But as a minimum level, this is the goal.

Let's say that you settle on 10,000 shares to be acquired over the course of 20 years. That would mean that you need to acquire 500 shares per year. Or put another way, you'd need to acquire 42 shares a month.

Or consider 5,000 shares acquired over the course of 30 years. That would mean buying 167 shares per year, or 14 shares a month.

You can also set your goals in terms of a fixed dollar investment per month. At a minimum, get started by investing $500 a month, or $1,000 a month. There are no set rules; you get started investing what you can and think about whether you want to do it by shares or by dollar amount.

A good way to do this is to keep a rule for at least one year. At the end of the year, you can re-evaluate your plan to see if it needs updating. If you are earning more money at the end of the year, you should update your plan to invest more money per month.

No matter what you do, you should stick to your plan. Discipline is going to be an important key to success when building a dividend investment portfolio. You are not going to achieve success if you fall off your plan repeatedly. People who end up with a nice retirement check are those who stick to regular investments made at regular intervals. The more discipline you have in sticking to your plan, the more likely it is that you are going to be able to achieve success.

Investing in Riskier Stocks

Some readers may be interested in investing in riskier stocks because, on a per-share basis, they are going to be cheaper. If you decide to do this, you will need to thoroughly investigate the company so that you can have a clear understanding of the risks that may be involved. The risk is whether or not the company has solid long term prospects. However, there are some that might be worthy of your consideration.

We aren't going to recommend any of these particular stocks, but you should be aware that they do exist and that they offer options worth considering, but a thorough investigation of the financial health of the company and its prospects in the coming years is important. Second, you should not put all of your money into one of these stocks. Diversification is very important for any stock portfolio, and if you are going to invest in one or more of these companies, you should not risk all of your money on it.

A "penny stock" is defined by the securities and exchange commission as any stock that trades at $5 or less per share. Due to inflation, the definition of "penny" has evolved since the 1920s.

Consolidated communications is a famous stock that pays a high dividend. This company provides communications infrastructure such as fiber optic communications. The company is actually an older firm, having been in business for more than 100 years. It's based in the Midwest, and the share price is only $5.24 a share. It's actually gone up about a dollar a share over the past month or so. The annual dividend is $1.55, giving a yield of $5.24. An investment of around $65,000 could generate an income of $20,000 a year from this stock. While this stock is a risk, you can take some comfort in the fact that the company has been around so long and it's always paid dividends. But that is no guarantee that it's going to survive in the future. One thing in its favor is the fact that it's involved in modern technology, so that might help it survive over the long term. However, a little research reveals that the stock is down 64% from its high for the year. Some investigation would be required to find out the reason, and whether or not the company has taken steps to address the issues.

Care must be used when considering companies like this. There are many to choose from, but you may be taking a large financial risk investing in them. But from time to time, you can find "hidden gems" that could turn out to be good investments.

Chapter 6:
Investment Strategies for
Dividend Stocks

At this point, you should have made up an investment plan. The investment plan seeks to establish the amount of money you want to make per year from dividends down the road when you have built up a substantial portfolio of investments. It starts there, and then the plan should include specific amounts of money or shares to buy each month in order actually to build up your portfolio.

Investment strategies are different. The purpose of a strategy is to follow some rules that are designed to build a safe portfolio that has some resistance to risk. There are a few different ways to do this, and the successful investor is going to use all of the strategies simultaneously, rather than trying to pick just one or two to use in your investment plan.

The main strategies that are used are going for growth or value stocks, or some mixture thereof. Using diversification, you don't have all your eggs in one basket. We will also talk about dollar-cost averaging, which helps you average out the money paid for shares so that you are not in a situation of buying too many shares at market highs. We will also talk about rebalancing at the end of each year to make sure that you are maintaining a portfolio that helps you reach your goals. Finally, we will talk about how to get out of an investment and why.

Growth vs. Value Stocks

A growth stock is a stock from a company that is expected to grow at a fast pace in the near future. In particular, a company that is a growth stock is one that is going to grow faster than the market average. The purpose of investing in a growth stock, at least in the next five years, and possibly more, is to take advantage of the capital appreciation of the shares. Examples of recent growth stocks include Netflix and Amazon.

Growth stocks don't typically pay dividends, although there are some notable exceptions. As we mentioned earlier in the book, many companies are seeking aggressive growth, and so they tend to reinvest all their profits rather than paying the profits out as dividends. Apple is one notable exception.

Growth stocks should not be confused with stocks that are dividend growth stocks. In the latter case, we are typically talking about a more stable and mature company that has a solid market share. It may be in a position of defending market share rather than trying to acquire it aggressively. A dividend growth stock is one that regularly increases their dividend payments.

Keep in mind that many dividend growth stocks are actually companies that do experience significant growth, even if they are not the highest growing companies in the market. Some examples of good companies that have seen solid growth in recent years are Microsoft, and Dollar General Corporation. And of course, we have already mentioned Apple.

When looking for a dividend growth stock, you want to look for a solid company that has shown increasing trends of paying higher dividends. We already mentioned that IBM had increased its dividend payment from $2 a year to more than $6 a year.

A value stock is usually one that is underpriced relative to the company's performance. To find a value stock, you compare its price to earnings ratio to similar companies in the same market. You want to make sure that you are comparing Apples to Apples, so if you are looking for a high tech value stock, you want to find one that has a low price to earnings ratio when compared to other companies that are in the same sector. So if you are looking at investing in a healthcare-related company, you should not compare its price to earnings ratio to Amazon or Netflix, you should compare it to other companies in the healthcare sector.

One of the goals of buying value stocks is seeing future capital appreciation. The belief is that since the price to earnings ratio is low, you are likely to see a significant increase in the stock price over the coming months and years, and so you are essentially in a situation where you can buy the stock at a discount, before a market adjustment brings the share price in line with that of other companies in the sector.

Looking for value stocks that pay dividends can be a good strategy, especially if the company is a more mature company, and therefore more stable. The goal of investing in mature companies is finding a firm that is able to weather the storms that come through the economy on a periodic basis. A mature company that is large in size is one that has gone through multiple recessions and come out of it all unscathed.

If you are investing in larger companies, if they are growth stocks or value stocks, it may not be all that important for your long term goals. Consider that companies like Apple can be solid investments over the long-term. Apple has shown a lot of capital appreciation and still pays dividends.

Dollar-Cost Averaging

The economy normally goes through cycles that include recessions. Sometimes, the recessions can be unusually deep and long. They are accompanied by a "bear" market, during which most stocks see declining share prices. Even when you are not in the midst of a bear market, stocks are going up and down in price all the time. These price movements have investors wondering when the best time is to buy a stock. It can be difficult, if not impossible, to determine the best time to buy shares of stock based on price. When you see the stock going down, you can sit waiting to by, and then you will see the price trend suddenly reverse. When that happens, you might miss out on the opportunity to buy at the best price.

Something important to realize is that unless you have amazing psychic powers, actually knowing when there is going to be a price reversal, or during a recession when the stock market will hit bottom, is something that impossible to predict. Even the best analysts and traders who have years of experience end up making the wrong estimates when it comes to figuring out when a real shift in market sentiment has occurred.

Of course, many investors make the mistake of always buying the stock at peak prices. Studies have shown that over long time periods, this actually doesn't hurt you as much as you think.

We can look at these facts and conclude that perhaps it is not really possible to pick the exact best time to buy shares. With that in mind, some smart people have figured out a simple way to buy shares without worrying about the current price, or whether or not you could be buying cheap shares or not. This method is called dollar-cost averaging.

The idea behind dollar-cost averaging is to buy stocks at regular intervals, regardless of the price per share paid. When you are doing this, you are not going to be worrying about whether or not the market is going up or down at any given time. Whether the market is a bull market or a bear market, this is of no consequence. The idea is to average out the prices that you are paying for your shares. Sometimes you are going to end up paying high prices for shares. But, if you follow a program of regular stock purchases at regular intervals, at other times you are going to be buying shares at discount prices. This takes out the guessing game of trying to figure out when the share price is going to drop, and whether or not a true "reversal" in trend is coming. Instead, your prices paid for the stock are going to basically average out. Sometimes they will be high, but those will be averaged out with the low prices paid during downturns.

If you look at any stock, you will notice that the charts are a bit erratic, even if you can pick out a larger trend. So if you buy shares using the dollar cost averaging method, you are going to be getting benefits from this at all times no matter what the larger trend is. You might, for example, be purchasing shares in the midst of an overall upward trend in price. However, on the way up in that trend, share prices are going to be going up and down on its way to the top, so at times if you are using dollar-cost averaging, you are going to be buying stocks at lower prices.

To set up a plan of dollar-cost averaging, you simply pick specific times during the month when you buy stocks, and you buy the stocks no matter what. So you should stop paying attention to the financial news, and not worry about what the latest fad is among traders. Stock traders are going to freak out over any news item that comes out, and prices may fluctuate quite a bit over time as a result. As a long-term investor using dollar-cost averaging as one of their strategies, you just shouldn't worry about this at all.

This is something that is going to take some discipline. The worry and stress people experience over bad news or the excitement that people feel when prices seem to be going up and up; these are natural emotions. You are going to feel these emotions, but part of the discipline of the dividend investor who is going to be successful is that you are going to ignore these feelings and the latest trend in the market.

People will panic when stock prices seem to be in free fall, but more than 100 years of data indicate something important—soon enough the price trend is going to reverse, and then prices will go up again. When prices are dropping, you might want to accelerate your purchases because you can get shares at discount prices. Then later, many years later, when you are living on your dividend income, the value of these shares will not only have recovered, they will be probably have gone up higher and be paying higher dividends.

So if you plan to do dollar-cost averaging, the minimal plan should be to purchase shares at regular intervals. If you are buying shares once a month, then make sure you always buy the shares on the same day each coming month. You can actually do better by purchasing shares once a week, rather than once a month. A good plan that you can use is to buy shares on every Monday. The particular day is not important, you can use every Wednesday if you want, or do every Friday. The point is to buy your shares once a week so that you are averaging out the changing stock prices over time.

Then be ready to move on buying even more shares if the stock has collapsed. When stock prices are dropping by a large amount, unless it is an unusual situation—say for example a company declaring bankruptcy or in some kind of legal trouble—buying shares when prices are dropping is a good strategy.

Diversification

No matter what stocks you settle on, even if they appear to be solid companies like Apple or IBM, diversification is going to be one of your most important strategies. The key behind diversification is that you are not riding all of your investment money on one company. In fact, a proper diversification plan is going to go a lot further than that. With a good diversification plan, you aren't just going to invest in three or four different companies. A true diversification plan should include 15 to 20 different companies in your portfolio.

In addition, diversification by a company is not enough to have a truly diversified portfolio. In fact, you should be diversifying by sector as well. There are many sectors in the stock market, from high tech to healthcare to utilities. As we will see later, you can also invest in energy and real estate for dividend income. These should be included as a part of your strategy for diversification as well.

When you are doing diversification, there is a balance between the number of companies you should have in your portfolio and the number that you can realistically have in the portfolio. If we lived in a perfect, ideal world, perhaps you could create a diversified portfolio with 100 different stocks. However, we don't live in such a world. Let me explain.

While you can say that the more stocks you have, the better when it comes to diversification, the reality is that the human mind can only wrap itself around a small number of companies. This is because you need to investigate and follow any companies that you invest in thoroughly. Most financial experts agree that more than 20 companies are too much for most people to follow. Even if you are a full-time investor and don't have to worry about a "day job," keeping track of more than 20 companies are going to be hard if not impossible to do.

On the other hand, we know that putting all of your investment money in a small number of companies, say less than seven, carries too much risk. This issue is even more important if you are the type of person that falls into the trap of investing in a set of companies that are in the same sector. This is actually a common problem. People gravitate toward certain areas, and so you might invest in all social media companies, for example. Or if you are fascinated by biotech, you might be the kind of person who only invests in pharmaceutical companies. This is problematic because entire sectors can see their own downturns while the rest of the market is doing well, or at least holding steady. So if you have everything invested in a single sector, you might find yourself in trouble while the rest of the market is going strong. But you won't have this problem if you make sure to invest in multiple sectors.

One way to ensure diversification is to invest in exchange traded funds. We will be covering this in detail in Chapter 5. There are many opportunities to expand your portfolio using exchange traded funds, and some investors might want to build up a portfolio that is entirely based on exchange traded funds.

Rebalancing Your Portfolio

As time goes on, some stocks are going to gain in value faster than others, and some are going to decrease in value. At the end of each year, it's a good time to have a detailed look at your portfolio and make adjustments. In some cases, if a stock is really underperforming, you might want to pull out of that stock altogether, if there are no signs that the stock is going to recover in the future. You can sell the shares and then reinvest the money in a more promising stock. Hopefully, the share value has not decreased so that you are taking losses, but if that is the case, you may want to consider getting out of the stock anyway. One of the mistakes that new investors make is they tend to stay in stock too long when the stock has crashed. They stay in the stock hoping that it's going to recover at some point, but then it never does. A good example is GE, which was once considered a prime investment. We can see that over five years, GE has languished. Even at the higher prices, it was already far down from its earlier peaks. Over the past two years, it dropped down and stayed down.

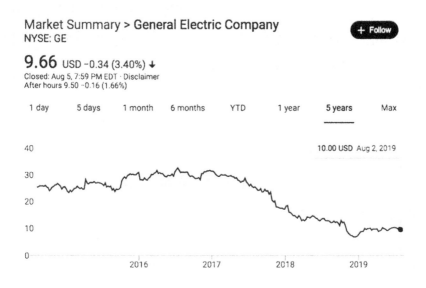

Now, none of them are psychic. The stock market can bring many surprises, so would you bet your life savings on GE suddenly turning around? You also can't bet your life savings that it's not going to turn around, and possibly regain some of its share value. But as a dividend investor, you are not a gambler. So looking at this stock, if it was in your portfolio, the smartest thing to do is to get out of the stock and find something that is better. Some may disagree. But if you get in a situation where you feel like you are "betting" or "hoping" for a stock to make a particular move, that is a sign that you should get out.

So part of rebalancing your portfolio is to get rid of stocks that are not helping you reach your goals because they are underperforming.

You should also use rebalancing to help keep the portfolio structured to reach your ultimate goals. So for a simple example, if you wanted a portfolio to have 60% of its value in stocks and 40% of its value in bonds, if the stocks went up in value over the past year so much that by December you have 70% of the value of the portfolio in stocks, it's time to rebalance if the 60/40 split is what you need to reach your goals. In this case, you would sell off shares of stock and then use the proceeds to invest in more bonds, until the 70/30 split was brought back into the 60/40 ratio.

This can be done with individual stocks as well. Suppose that you have a portfolio that has 25% invested in high-tech, 25% in the healthcare sector, 25% in manufacturing, and 25% in financial companies. At the end of the year, the high-tech sector might have grown so that now you have 50% in high tech, 12% in manufacturing, 20% in financial companies, and 18% in healthcare. In this case, you would sell off some of your high-tech stocks and then use the proceeds to buy stocks in the other sectors to bring it back into the 25-25-25-25 balance that you started off with.

This is the main way that people rebalance their portfolios at the end of each year. You only need to do this once per year.

Chapter 7:
Investing Using Funds

In the last chapter, one of the main strategies that we discuss was diversification. One of the things that was mentioned is that the more you diversify, the better. That is because diversification protects you from the inevitable downturns that one or more stocks in your portfolio are going to experience at some point. So imagine that you have a portfolio with five stocks in it. If two of them go under, that means you have lost a substantial proportion of your investment. On the other hand, if you had 20 stocks and two of them went down, you can see that the overall consequences to your portfolio would have been minimized.

As we mentioned in the last chapter, you could take that even further. Imagine, instead of 20 stocks, you have your investment distributed across 100 or even more stocks. In that case, you would have a maximally protected portfolio. And the matter which direction the market goes, you know that not all those 100 companies are going to make it over the long-term. But having a widely diversified portfolio means that most of your investments will come out intact and some of them will grow more than others making up for the losses.

But as we mentioned, there is a limit to what the human mind can handle unless you happen to be a professional investor. Most readers of this book are not going to have the ability to work full time on managing their stock portfolio. And as we also mentioned, as a result of this, most experts feel that having maybe 20 stocks is the maximum that an individual investor should keep in their portfolio.

But as some of you know, there is another way to approach investing. This is through the use of funds. There are two basic types of funds that you can use. These are mutual funds and exchange traded funds. Our preference is for exchange traded funds for reasons that will become clear as we go through the chapter. However, mutual funds came first, and so we are going to explain the concept of a fund using mutual funds before we get to exchange traded funds.

Either way, the main benefit of using funds for investing is that you get automatic diversity. Some funds track major stock indexes. But there are all kinds of funds the track everything from metals to real estate to energy. So it's entirely possible to build up a nicely diversified portfolio that focuses on multiple sectors of the economy as well as giving you investments in multiple stocks.

Of course, many people actually enjoy picking individual stocks to invest in. But once again, there are no either-or scenarios when it comes to investing. So just because you are investing in funds, that doesn't mean that you can't still devote some of your investment money to picking individual stocks. The way that your portfolio is ultimately set up is going to be a personal choice. When we start looking at some of the exchange traded funds that are available, you are going to see that many of them are suitable for reaching the goals that you probably have when it comes to dividend investing. Therefore, the details of how your portfolio is set up are going to be entirely up to you. Some people may choose to go entirely with funds, while others won't like the style and so they will stick with picking individual stocks. But there is a possibility of going in between. So you can say devote 40% of your portfolio to individual stocks, and then devote 60% to exchange traded funds of various types. Or instead, you may devote 70% in individual stocks and 30% to exchange traded funds. There is no right answer to this question, and you will have to decide how to set this up yourself depending on how much risk you want to put in individual stocks or how risk-averse you are and so more likely to choose fund type investing.

Mutual Funds

So what is a fund? Let's imagine an investor named Bob. Let's say Bob got a brilliant idea when he was trying to invest in stocks. It occurred to Bob that one of the best ways to invest in the market would be to invest in all 500 companies of the S&P 500. Bob tries to do this, buying one share at a time. Pretty soon and he realized that for one investor, this was simply an impossible task. He simply couldn't come up with enough capital to do it.

So what was the idea that Bob actually came up with? Bob realized that he could approach 10 of his friends and suggest to them that they pool their money together into a fund. That way, Bob would have 10 times the buying power than he would have by himself.

So let's say that Bob's friends put in $1 million each to create this fund. Now, Bob has $11 million including his own portion, to invest in the 500 stocks that make up the S&P 500. In return for their investments, Bob followed the model of a company issuing stock. So he divided up the $11 million dollars into pieces that he called units. He was careless with his language, so sometimes he just called them shares thinking about the stock market in general. Then, he made each share for the unit worth $100. So for each of his friends at putting $1 million, he gave them 10,000 shares in the fund. Since the fund was put together for the benefit of all the investors, he said it was mutual. And thus Bob invented the mutual fund.

Each night, Bob would buy and sell shares in order to keep the fund as profitable as possible. Bob started getting more sophisticated in his approach. He thought that by rebalancing his investments to emphasize growth stocks, he could make his fund grow at a faster rate each year damn the S&P 500 actually grew. In order to be compensated for this extra work that he was putting in, Bob charged his investors a small fee.

Of course, the story is fictitious. But it gives you a basic idea of what a mutual fund is. It is simply a pooled amount of money collected from multiple investors. Of course, a real mutual fund is going to have a lot more money than just $10 million. But the concept is basically the same.

Types of Mutual Funds

Mutual funds don't have to invest in stocks. In fact, there're many types of mutual funds. Stock funds are the most common or well-known types of mutual funds. Within the category of stock funds, there is a wide range of options available. So, for example, you can invest in mutual funds that focus only on growth stocks. The goal of such fun would be to get financial gains via capital appreciation that beat the market average.

Other funds may specialize in different industries segments or sectors. One of the most popular types of mutual funds is those that track a stock market index. Just like in our example above, there are many mutual funds and exchange traded funds that track the S&P 500. You can also find funds that track the Dow Jones industrial average, NASDAQ, or the Russell 3000.

Some mutual funds only invest in stocks that pay dividends. But as we will see later, many different types of funds will pay dividends.

There are other types of investments that can be made through mutual funds and also by using exchange traded funds as well. For example, you can invest in a money market fund, which might be a mixture of investments in US government bonds, municipal bonds, and banking investments. Bond mutual funds will invest in different types of corporate bonds, in these may be of higher risk, but they pay higher interest rates. The risk to the individual investor is actually going to be relatively low. This is because each fund is going to invest in hundreds or thousands of individual securities.

Mutual funds tend to be professionally managed. A fund manager is going to pick the securities that are in each fund. As time goes on, the fund manager may buy and sell shares as they see fit in order to try and keep the fun performing at a high-level. Some people who don't want to get too deeply involved in the stock market, like the fact that the mutual fund is professionally managed. The way they see it that way, they can avoid getting too deeply involved in investing. For whatever reason, they may not want to be actively involved in managing their stocks and other investments.

Mutual funds have many downsides, however. One of the downsides is that this professional management comes with a price. Many mutual funds charged a large number of fees that can add up over time, and cut into your profits. Another downside of mutual funds is that they only trade once a day after the market close. So if you see a big move in the stock market, whether it's a big uptick in price or a meltdown, when you are in a mutual fund, you cannot respond to that big change until after market close. Of course, you can call in your order or place it online, but it's not going to execute until after the market has closed.

Some mutual funds also charged expensive fees called loads. What this amounts to is you are charged a commission every time you purchase or sell shares. So to use a specific example, if you invested thousand dollars in a mutual fund but it had a 5% load, that would mean that you would actually only be putting $950 into your investment, well the fund would take $50 off the top as a fee. Honestly, this is hard to swallow in today's world. You can find an exchange traded fund that will track nearly the same investments as any mutual fund, and you can actually buy shares of the exchange traded fund with zero commissions charged by the brokerage. One brokerage to charges zero commissions on all exchange traded funds is Robin Hood. There are also some others that you can look into.

If you dig around mutual funds, you are going to see that Psalm advertise themselves as no-load funds. These types of mutual funds don't charge the sales fee known as the load. However, these funds may still charge other fees. And in fact, funds that charge a load may charge fees on top of the load as well. When you research mutual funds, you can look up all the fees that they charge which must be disclosed in the prospectus.

Almost no-load mutual funds are going to have specific requirements for you to invest. For example, they might require that you keep your money in the fund for a specified number of years. Mutual funds may also have requirements for an initial amount invested. So this could preclude small investors who are just starting out from getting involved with mutual funds.

So to summarize, Mutual funds have several benefits. These include strong diversification and exposure to many different sectors. Mutual funds also allow you to invest in multiple types of financial securities such as bonds. However, Mutual funds have lots of downsides. The main downsides include having to wait until after market close to trade shares, and, lots of fees and sales commissions. You may also face the problem of having to invest a minimum amount of capital in order to get started.

What is an Exchange Traded Fund?

Of course, many people notice the downsides of mutual funds through the years. So it's no surprise that overtime, some people thought of taking the good characteristics of mutual funds and creating a different type of fund that got rid of the downsides. This was the birth of the exchange traded fund.

The first thing to consider is the weakness of mutual funds caused by the fact that they are not traded during the day. So imagine that the stock market suddenly had a rally. You might want to get in on more shares. Or alternatively, the stock market might be crashing, and at 10:00 AM, you decide you want to get out. The problem is that with a mutual fund, your orders will not be taken care of until after the market close. And who knows how much money you might miss out on or lose as a result of the time delay.

So the first change that was made was to create a fund that was set up in the same way as a mutual fund in that it was very diverse. However, the exchange traded fund, as the name suggests, is actually traded in real-time on the stock markets. So while an exchange traded fund cannot be said to be stock because it's not an investment in a single company, exchange traded funds offer shares that are traded exactly like stocks. So these are listed on the stock market exchange with a ticker, and you can buy and sell as many shares that you want, and you can do it when you want. That is you can trade these during the times that the market is open.

Another benefit is that exchange traded funds have no minimum investment required other than the price required to buy at least one share. So while some mutual fund might require you to put in $5000 just to enter the door, if you only wanted to spend $85 dollars to buy into an exchange traded fund by purchasing a single share, you could actually do that. And two hours later, if you are tired of it or think you made a mistake, you could sell that share.

Exchange traded funds also dispense with all the fees that are associated with mutual funds. There may be some small amount of fees that are charged, but frankly, they're tiny compared to those charged by mutual funds. So trading exchange traded funds boils down to something that really isn't all that different then trading shares of Facebook or Apple. If you invest $1000, you are basically going to be investing $1000. It's not going to be like a loaded mutual fund that takes off a fee off the top.

And as we've noted, since exchange traded funds are traded like stocks, if there is a large market move during the day, you can take full advantage of it. You can also buy options against exchange traded funds and trade them. Options are beyond the scope of this book, and so we are not going to discuss the details, but some of the most popular options are in fact options traded on exchange traded funds.

ETFs Have Diversification

As far as the way the investments are made, exchange traded funds are quite similar to mutual funds. So a large amount of money is pulled together and used to purchase shares of stock. So if you were to buy shares in an exchange traded fund that tracks the S&P 500, you would be buying stock in all 500 companies. Exchange traded fund is able to do this because they have a large pool of money collected from thousands or more investors. In fact, some of the most popular and highly traded financial instruments today our exchange traded funds.

The first exchange traded funds came on the market roughly 30 years ago. Since that time, they have exploded in popularity and in the number of funds that are available. Basically, anything that you could possibly think of investing in has an exchange traded fund associated with it. So there are exchange traded funds that track all the major stock indexes, there are exchange traded funds that track precious metals, and you can also invest in funds that track real estate, energy, commercial real estate, healthcare sector, and many other areas.

For the purposes of dividend and investing, exchange traded funds make an excellent addition to your portfolio. In fact, it would be completely reasonable to only invest in exchange traded funds. Or as we mentioned in the introduction, you could develop a broad portfolio that was some mixture of exchange traded funds and individual stocks.

But when you start investigating this, you are going to find that there are many exchange traded funds that actually paid dividends. What happens is they will collect dividends from all the investments of the fund. And then you as the investor we'll be paid a dividend payment that is in proportion to your share in the fund.

In many index funds on the yield may not be quite as high as it is with some individual stocks. However, it's still going to be relatively competitive, and you can invest in many index funds that have yields that are similar to those seen by Apple. We just mentioned Apple again to use it as an example.

However, unlike investing in Apple by itself, when you invest in exchange traded funds, you are investing in hundreds of companies at once. When you buy a share of the exchange traded fund, you are basically buying a tiny fraction of the share of some of the companies that are represented by the fund.

Another advantage that exchange traded funds have with respect to mutual funds is higher liquidity. Mutual funds are relatively liquid. You can sell your shares and cash out usually later in the day. However, remember that you can only trade mutual funds after the trading day has ended. In contrast, since you can trade exchange traded funds at any time, that basically means that exchange traded funds are super liquid. In fact, you can even day trade an exchange traded funds.

Using ETFs to Earn Income from Non-Stock Securities

Exchange-traded funds are like mutual funds in the sense that you can use them to invest in practically anything. So when you start digging around, you are not only going to find that exchange traded funds are available for a given stock or index, you are also going to notice that you can invest in gold or gold mining, or you can invest in high yield bonds for example. The possibilities are quite endless, and for this reason, a lot of people only invest in exchange traded funds.

Examples of Dividend-Paying ETFs

There are many ETFs that pay dividends. The way this is handled is the ETF collects all the dividends from dividend-paying stocks in the fund, and then it divides those up on a per-share basis. So, let us imagine that we had a simple exchange traded fund that had 100 stocks in the fund. Furthermore, for simplicity, we will imagine that there are 100 shares of stock in the fund.

If 50 of the stocks paid a $2 dividend, the total dividend payment would be $100. This would then be divided by the total number of shares, which in this case is 100. So we have a payment of $100/(100 shares) = $1/share.

One of the most popular exchange traded funds is SPY, which invests in the S&P 500. The annualized dividend payout for SPY is $5.73. That gives a yield of about 2%, with a share price of $283 at the time of writing.

That is a pretty good example. While the yield is a bit lower, you can see that the actual payment per share is quite comparable to IBM. Moreover, the growth of SPY year over year tends to be quite good, and so you will get some pretty good capital appreciation on your shares.

To see another example, we can look at QQQ, which tracks the NASDAQ 100. The annual dividend payment, in this case, is much smaller, at $1.66 per share. This gives a yield of 0.92%.

We've already mentioned VYM, which is the Vanguard High Dividend Yield fund. The yield is around 3%, with an annual payout of $2.50. The share price for this one is only $84 a share, so it is worth looking into since it will be easier to amass a larger amount of shares.

A better option, however, which is in the same price range per share at $96, is the iShares Select Dividend ETF. This fund invests in companies that have a solid five-year history of paying dividends. The annual dividend for this fund is $3.53, with a yield of 3.7%.

PGX is an exchange traded fund that invests in preferred stock. Preferred stock is not offered by most companies, but it's a type of stock designed to give you a preferred spot in line if you will when being able to collect on the debts of a company that goes bankrupt. So you will be first in line after the creditors that the company owes money to. Some stocks that offer preferred shares include Bank of America, Allstate, and John Hancock. Preferred stock does not convey voting rights as common stock does.

PGX has a dividend payment of $2.98 and a yield of around 2.6%.

Chapter 8:

Growing an IRA Using Dividend Payments

If you have invested in an individual retirement account or IRA, one of the constraints that you have probably noticed is that you can only invest about $5,500 per year into the account. This constraint can restrict the amount of money you can build up in the IRA, especially if you are an older investor who hasn't been saving money up to this point. The government does allow you to put in a little bit extra as "catch up" money if you are over the age of 50. However, it's not very much money. The reason that there are these constraints on individual retirement accounts is that they have certain tax advantages, so that is part of the trade-off. In order to get the tax advantages, you have to accept the lower contribution amounts.

But dividends can come to the rescue here. That is because although you are limited in the sizes of contributions that you can put in an IRA, the amount of money inside the IRA has no limitations on growth.

As a result, one strategy people use to grow their IRA faster than it would grow otherwise is to buy dividend stocks inside the IRA. Then you can use the power of compound interest inside the IRA to make it grow faster. You can do this by using the dividend payments to reinvest inside the account. If you use this process for several years, then at the end you are going to own far more shares of stock than you could have possibly purchased had you just stuck to the allowed contribution limits.

Traditional or Roth IRA

For people who aren't familiar with the concept of an IRA, there are two types of individual retirement accounts. There are traditional individual retirement accounts and Roth individual retirement accounts. For both types of IRAs, you can only contribute $5,500 per year if you are under the age of 50, and you can contribute $6,500 per year if you are over the age of 50. For a married couple that files their taxes jointly, they are allowed to make the full contribution to a Roth IRA if their income is $184,000 or lower. For a taxpayer who files as a single individual, the full contribution is allowed only if your income is $117,000 or lower.

If you can't meet these income requirements and still want to contribute the full amount, then you are going to have to use a traditional IRA. The differences between the two types of IRAs go beyond this. A Roth IRA is funded with after-tax money. It can compound or grow inside the IRA tax-free, and when you make withdrawals from the IRA after retirement, the money you take out is tax-free.

In contrast, a traditional IRA is funded with money that isn't taxed now, but you will pay taxes on the money when you take it out of the account. There are no income limitations for a traditional IRA. So that is one major difference between the two accounts, the second is that a Roth IRA will result in no taxes on the money pulled out down the road, so it's a bet that it's better to pay taxes now. A traditional IRA is a bet that it is better to pay taxes in the future. Of course, if you surpass the income limitations of the Roth, you are stuck using the traditional IRA.

Using Dividend Stocks in a Roth IRA

With a Roth individual retirement account, you pay taxes on the money used to invest now, but once inside the account and later when you make withdrawals, the money is tax-free. The strategy to use to grow your IRA faster than it would with the maximum contribution that the law allows is to use DRIPs inside the Roth IRA. So when you receive your dividend payments, if you are using DRIPs, then the money will be automatically invested to purchase more shares of stock.

The dividend income that you earn inside the Roth IRA is not counted toward your annual contribution limit, and you are not taxed on it. The ideal strategy for a Roth IRA is to invest in quality stocks that rather than paying the highest dividends, are stocks that are also good growth stocks. So you will benefit from the capital appreciation of the shares, including the additional shares that you will be purchasing every time that dividends are paid.

This means that the strategy used when buying dividends inside an IRA is going to be a different strategy generally used for dividend-paying stocks. With dividend-paying stocks, the investor seeks to generate an income from the dividends at some point. When you are buying dividend-paying stocks inside an IRA account, your goal is actually to purchase more shares than you would have been able to purchase otherwise. So the goal is to accumulate more shares of stock, which will help you grow the IRA account faster.

When you make withdrawals from the Roth IRA, if you meet certain conditions, you can withdraw the money from the account after age 59 ½ tax-free. The conditions that you must meet is that you have had the Roth IRA for at least five years prior to making withdrawals and that you satisfy the age requirement. If your age is below 59 ½, you will have to pay income tax on the contributions that you are withdrawing and capital gains on the dividend income.

Traditional IRA

If you have a traditional IRA, you should use the same strategy for the purpose of growing your account. However, you are not going to see any tax advantages. When you have a traditional IRA, you are not taxed on the money at the time you contribute it, but you are taxed when you take it out of the account. This holds true for any money earned inside the IRA, including dividend payments. When you take them out, you are going to have to pay ordinary income tax on them.

The Magnifying Power of Dividend Stocks in a Retirement Account

Each time that you earn dividends, and they are used to buy more shares of stock, that means in the next quarter, you are going to earn that many more dividend payments. Then the next time you get a larger dividend payment from the increased number of shares you have, and these, in turn, can be reinvested to buy yet more shares of stock, increasing the number of shares paying dividends the following quarter and so on.

Chapter 9:
Special Dividend Investments

Large corporations are not the only ways that you can build up a good dividend income. There are many specialized types of investments that you can take advantage of to not only add some diversity to your portfolio by gaining exposure to other industries but also to get some major tax advantages. There are three classes of investments that are worth considering. These include REITs, or Real Estate Investment Trusts, Master Limited Partnerships, and Business Development Companies.

These types of organizations are publicly traded on the stock markets, so you can buy shares and invest in them just like you would for stocks associated with major companies like Apple or Facebook. However, the tax treatment of your income from these companies might be a little bit different, but as we will see, there can be advantages as well.

Real Estate Investment Trusts

The first major class of companies that are great for getting regular dividend income are known as Real Estate Investment Trusts, or REITs. These companies are involved in different types of real estate holdings. But don't be fooled by the term "real estate." Although many of them hold properties that you would commonly associate with the term, there are several different REITS that hold unusual properties that you may not have ever thought about as a possible way to invest.

Some real estate investment trusts are pretty conventional, holding residential and commercial properties. For example, you can invest in a company that holds large numbers of single-family homes or apartments that it rents out. Many firms are involved in commercial real estate, such as renting out hotels, motels, office buildings, nursing homes, and other commercial properties. It may surprise you to learn that major hotel chains like Marriott often don't own the properties they use, instead, they will rent them from a real estate investment trust.

Other real estate investment trusts are surprisingly unconventional and involved with cutting edge technology. For example, there are several that own cell phone towers and other communications infrastructure. This can be an excellent investment since it's pretty clear that cell phones are not going anywhere in the near future, so your investment is likely pretty secure.

Other REITs own properties, such as cloud-based computing banks. Large corporations rent these from the real estate trust, and this is another area of high-tech that is going to be very solid in the coming years.

Real Estate Investment trusts are a special type of entity that was created by Congress in the early 1980s, along with the other types of organizations described in this chapter. The key factor for a REIT is that it owns property that produces income, so it's basically any type of property that can be leased or rented to others.

REITs are structured to avoid tax liability to the company. In order to do this, they must meet certain requirements. The main requirement that they have to satisfy is that 90% of the profits the company makes are passed on to shareholders. This fact makes them very attractive to investors, and they often produce very high returns.

If you are going to invest in REITs, like anything else, the key is diversification and evaluating the financial health of the company. Since they are traded on major stock exchanges, the financial statements of the company are made publicly available. So before investing in a REIT, you should do the same type of fundamental analysis that you would do with any other company.

According to the website REIT.com, REITs in the United States have a market capitalization of more than a trillion dollars. The types of REITS available cover 13 different sectors. These include office buildings, industrial REITS (warehouses, manufacturing facilities), retail (shopping malls), Lodging (hotels and motels), Residential (single-family homes, apartments), Timberland (property that has trees for harvesting for lumber needs), Self-Storage Facilities, Healthcare (hospitals, old age homes, rehabilitation centers, etc.), infrastructure (fiber optic cables, cell phone towers, pipelines), Data Centers, and diversified REITs that hold multiple types of properties.

REITs often provide high yields and also solid capital appreciation. Dividends and yields are comparable to those found in many stocks.

Most of the time, the income you receive from REITs are going to be taxed as ordinary income. They are classified as non-qualified dividends. The only capital gains taxes you would incur will be if you sell your shares in REITs for a gain.

Master Limited Partnerships

Master Limited Partnerships, or MLPs, are another specially created category of businesses created by Congress. MLPs are usually associated with energy production from oil and natural gas. Generally speaking, energy production is divided into three different "streams." The upstream part of energy production is the actual drilling for oil and natural gas. Mid-stream is the transport, storage, and possibly refining of oil and natural gas. This can include storage facilities, pipelines, ships, or trucks used to move oil and natural gas from one place to another or to store it at port facilities. Finally, downstream services are those that get the product directly to customers. Some companies are involved in all three levels. Master Limited Partnerships are mid-stream energy companies.

So if you invest in an MLP, this is going to be an investment in a company that might own storage facilities, pipelines, and the like. Similar to REITs, these companies are required to pass on most of their profits as dividend payments. They also trade on the major stock exchanges.

Unlike REITs, however, MLPs offer an unprecedented opportunity when it comes to tax purposes. The name of these types of entities is a giveaway. It's a partnership, rather than a corporation and as an investor, you become a limited partner.

The company is managed by a general partner who is paid for their services, but like REITs, MLPS are required to pass on 90% of their profits to investors. However, the fact that you are legally considered a partner in the company changes things considerably. Not only do you get profits paid out as healthy dividends, depreciation expenses for the company are also passed on. As you might imagine, depreciation expenses for thinks like oil tanks and pipelines can be quite substantial.

The result of this is that you are probably going to be able to deduct a large fraction of your income from the MLP. It is suggested that typically you will only pay income tax on 10% of your returns. For this reason, many investors like investing in MLPs. You can find lists of MLPs to invest in on dividend.com.

Business Development Companies

The next type of investment we are going to consider is another entity set up to pass on most of its profits to investors called a Business Development Company. In short, these types of companies provide financing to other businesses. They can play a role similar to venture capitalist investors or provide loans and financing to businesses that need it. They typically target small to mid-sized companies. Sometimes, they will specifically target financially distressed companies that need capital.

Business Development Companies, or BDCs as they are sometimes known, are publicly held companies that are traded on the major stock exchanges. Their income is distributed to investors in the form of dividends. Congress created this category of company in order to help small and mid-sized businesses raise capital. There are a small number of these available on the major stock exchanges that you can invest in.

Many dividend investors like BDCs because they offer the opportunity to get high yields. There is also a chance to benefit from an increase in share price, and you can possibly profit from higher dividends down the road as a result, or you can sell your shares for a gain.

Tax-wise, the dividend payments that you receive from a business development company are going to be considered ordinary income. That is because the dividend income these companies provide is considered to be non-qualified dividends. However, many investors are still drawn to them because of the high yields that some of these companies offer.

Other Income Generating Investments

Receiving dividend payments is not the only way to generate income from your investment activities. However, sticking to the stock market, we are going to consider using exchange-traded funds to make other types of investments. Specifically what we have in mind is using exchange traded funds to invest in U.S. Treasuries, municipal bonds, corporate bonds, and money market funds. As far as the fund is concerned, these are income-generating vehicles that will pay interest to the fund.

However, exchange traded funds are stocks. So for the investor, the earnings from these investments are going to be paid out as dividends. This allows you to gain different types of investment exposure while adding to your dividend portfolio.

A Wall Street company that offers several exchange traded funds called SPDR has several that you can use to earn income from corporate bonds. These are known as the Barclay's Bond ETFs because they track a particular bond index that goes by this name.

CWB is the Barclay's Capital Convertible Bond ETF. This fund is trading at $52 a share and has a yield of 1.86%. The annualized dividend payout is $0.97 a share. For a more lucrative fund that generates income from corporate bonds, consider JNK, which holds multiple "junk" bonds. These types of bonds are issued by companies that have had credit problems in the past. As a result, they pay higher interest rates. As an investor, your risk is limited because JNK has holdings in a large number of companies, so if one defaults you are unlikely to be impacted by it, and the managers of the fund may be swapping companies in and out as they deem appropriate in order to keep the performance of the fund at high levels. The yield on this fund is 5.56%, with an annual payout of $5.98. It is trading at $107 per share.

If you would like to get some exposure to bonds issued by the federal government, there are many options available that target different types of bonds with different maturities. One example is the Vanguard Long-Term Treasury ETF, which trades on the stock exchange as VGLT. The dividend yield is 2.49%, with an annualized payout of $2.13 per share. The share price is $85 per share.

Many investors might find these numbers disappointing but consider two things. The first is that unlike putting your money in the bank, as we mentioned early on in the book, the asset itself is appreciating in many cases. That is the share prices of the fund or stock you are investing in is probably increasing over longer-term time periods. So you are going to be taking advantage of this either by selling the shares at some point or through higher per share dividend payments as a result of an attempt to keep yields constant.

Second, the values quoted here are actually comparable to many stocks. Consider Apple, which is paying an annual dividend of $3 a share, but whose yield is only 1.6%. That can help to put things in perspective when you are considering other types of income-generating investments.

Exchange traded funds also provide an opportunity to earn dividend payments from other types of bonds. Many investors used to favor municipal bonds for tax reasons, but another reason to consider municipal bonds is that they are highly reliable. This is because they are backed by the taxation power of the government agency that issues them. A company that offers exchange traded funds called iShares has several municipal bond funds.

One example is MAYHX, which is a high yield municipal bond fund. One advantage of these types of funds is they provide good capital appreciation as well. The year to date return on this fund is 8%, which is a figure that often beats the stock market average. The yield for this fund is 3.87%.

Many investors like to balance their portfolios between stocks and strictly income generating assets. Although exchange traded funds are considered to be stocks when investing in funds that are used to invest in bonds, you can stay in the stock market but balance your portfolio as you see fit. The general advice is to move to safer investments as people age, but keep in mind that this kind of advice is usually meant to address the situation where people are investing in aggressive growth based portfolios, and so they are not seeking out stocks that pay dividends.

Money Market ETFs

You can also make your overall exposure more diversified using money market ETFs. Typically, these have a wide diversity of investments in different government and corporate bonds, and also in cash. One example is the JP Morgan Ultra-Short Income ETF. The year to date return on this type of fund is going to be modest, and quite a bit lower than the stock market average most of the time. However, it will offer you an income-generating investment that also gives you some security in case there is a stock market downturn. The yield for this fund is about 2.6% and its trading at $50 a share. About 64% of the fund is in cash investments. The rest is divided between U.S. government debt and corporate debt.

Many Options

As you can see from this discussion, there are many options to consider when building an investment portfolio that gives you an income from dividends. You can make your portfolio quite diverse. One of the nice things about these other possibilities is that they trade on the stock market. This allows you to get exposure to real estate, energy, finance, cash, and bonds without having actually to invest in all these different markets.

However, I recommend keeping things simple. You don't want to go overboard and invest in so many different areas that it's impossible to keep track of them all. Therefore the original recommendation of 15-20 different investments is probably good to stick too even if all of those are not individual stocks. How you allocate everything is going to be a personal decision, but I would put about half in the stock market, invest in a few REITs and MLPs, and then maybe have 3-5 exchange traded funds that invested in bonds and other types of income generating assets. Some stock investments can be in ETFs that track different sectors or indexes. They all don't have to be put in individual stocks.

Some people will find the idea of REITs and MLPs very intriguing, however, and you can even build up your entire portfolio using these types of investments. The tax sheltering possibilities of income from MLPs is of particular interest.

For many investors, getting the highest possible income is going to be the goal, so with that in mind, you can always seek out the highest yields and worry about that rather than what type of investment you are getting involved with. But in any case, don't put all of your eggs in one basket.

Conclusion

Dividend investing is a great way to grow your wealth and build a portfolio of income-generating assets that can bring you and your family income for the rest of your life. If you go about your investing methodically and carefully, at the end of your investment phase, you will be able to build up a strong portfolio than can produce significant levels of income. How high that income turns out to be will depend on many factors, including the growth of the company, how much you invest, and how regularly you invest.

Keep in mind that normally, this type of investment strategy takes time to build up. Most of us are not walking around with a million dollars lying around, so the earlier that you start planning to build up a dividend investment portfolio, the better off you are going to be. That doesn't mean that late starters can't take advantage of this too, but if you are a late investor, you are going to have to put a lot more capital into your investing and proceed aggressively. Generally speaking, at a minimum, a ten-year time horizon is required, with a range of 15-30 years in most cases. But don't let any fixed rules discourage you, put what you can when you can if you are a late investor.

Using an IRA is one way to grow your investments. Dividends allow you to invest in these retirement vehicles and go beyond the usual contribution limits. Normally, you can only put between $5,500 to $6,500 per year into an IRA, but if you are able to use dividend reinvestment plans, you can grow your IRA on steroids.

There are many different securities that can pay dividends. At the top, we have large corporations that pay dividends, which is what most people think about when they consider income investing in stocks. But as we've seen, you can also generate income using mutual and exchange traded funds. There are also ample opportunities for investments and profits, including dividend income from REITs, Master Limited Partnerships, and Business Development Companies.

No matter which path you take, the fact that you are taking control of your own financial situation puts you in a far better position than most.

Thank you again for downloading this book. I hope that you have found it helpful and informative. Please be sure to leave a review for us!

Other books of the Autor Patrick Neilson:

☑ Option trading for beginners

☑ Stock Market Investing for beginners

☑ Swing Trading

Made in the USA
Monee, IL
20 February 2020